WOMAN

thou art
HEALED *&* WHOLE

A 90 Day Devotional Journey

DESTINY IMAGE BOOKS BY T.D. JAKES

WOMAN

thou art

HEALED & WHOLE

A 90 Day Devotional Journey

T.D. JAKES

DESTINY IMAGE® PUBLISHERS, INC.

P.O. Box 310, Shippensburg, PA 17257-0310

"Promoting Inspired Lives."

This book and all other Destiny Image and Destiny Image Fiction books are available at Christian bookstores and distributors worldwide.

Material included from previously published book, *Woman Thou Art Loosed*.

Cover design by: Eileen Rockwell

For more information on foreign distributors, call 717-532-3040.

Reach us on the Internet: www.destinyimage.com.

ISBN 13 HC: 978-0-7684-0979-6

ISBN 13 eBook: 978-0-7684-0980-2

For Worldwide Distribution, Printed in the U.S.A.

15 / 22 21 20

INTRODUCTION

God wants His daughters to be *healed* and *whole*. Unfortunately, so many women miss out on receiving this divine inheritance. *Why*?

This is not due to unwillingness from God's end, but rather unwillingness on ours to embrace the *journey*. Miracles happen instantly; healing takes time. It's often a journey, not a quick fix. Be it physical or emotional healing, there is often a process that one needs to submit to in order to experience the full healing provision that Jesus made available.

Woman Thou Art Loosed is a powerful declaration of freedom that is truly timeless. The same Son of God who spoke these healing words to the woman with a spirit of infirmity in Luke 13 is the One who definitively stated, *"So if the Son sets you free, you will be free indeed"* (John 8:36 NIV). Paul expands on this, explaining that *"it is for freedom that Christ has set us free. Stand firm, then, and do not let yourselves be burdened again by a yoke of slavery"* (Gal. 5:1 NIV).

Jesus Christ came to set you free in every area of your life. He provides the holistic healing ointment that brings restoration to your body, soul, and spirit.

Take the next 90 days and receive His healing work. Don't rush it. Don't approach this devotional like another book that you need to breeze through in order to get on to the next thing. Each of the 90 entries is specifically provided to lead you on a powerful healing journey.

God does not want to give you a quick fix so you feel better for a season but end up back in the same destructive cycles as yesterday. He wants you loosed. He wants you free. He wants you un-entangled, where no snare can restrain you and no scheme of the enemy can hold you back from fulfilling your divine destiny.

Jesus did not come to provide a bandage for your bondage; He wants you free *indeed!*

FOR EVERY PROBLEM THERE IS A PRESCRIPTION

And when Jesus saw her, he called her to him, and said unto her, Woman, thou art loosed from thine infirmity.
—LUKE 13:12

The Holy Spirit periodically lets us catch a glimpse of the personal testimony of one of the patients of the Divine Physician Himself. This woman's dilemma is her own, but perhaps you will find some point of relativity between her case history and your own. She could be like someone you know or have known; she could even be like you.

There are three major characters in this story. These characters are the person, the problem, and the prescription. It is important to remember that for every person, there will be a problem. Even more importantly, for every problem our God has a prescription!

Jesus's opening statement to the problem in this woman's life is not a recommendation for counseling—it is a challenging command! Often much more is involved in maintaining deliverance than just discussing past trauma. Jesus did not counsel what should have been commanded. I am not, however, against seeking the counsel of godly people. On the contrary, the Scriptures say:

> *Blessed is the man that walketh not in the counsel of the ungodly, nor standeth in the way of sinners, nor sitteth in the seat of the scornful* (Psalm 1:1).

> *Where no counsel is, the people fall: but in the multitude of counsellors there is safety* (Proverbs 11:14).

What I want to make clear is that after you have analyzed the condition, after you have understood its origin, it will still take the authority of God's Word to put the past under your feet! This woman was suffering as a result of something that attacked her 18 years earlier. I wonder if you can relate to the long-range aftereffects of past pain? This kind of trauma is as fresh to the victim today as it was the day it occurred. Although the problem may be rooted in the past, the prescription is a present word from God!

YOUR HEALING JOURNEY

Remember that for every problem you face, Heaven has a divine prescription.

God has a command of authority that you can bring against your present condition!

IDENTIFY YOUR INFIRMITY

Woman, thou art loosed from thine infirmity.
—LUKE 13:12

Jesus Christ is the Word of God, and the Word is the same yesterday, today, and forevermore (see Heb. 13:8)! That is to say, the word you are hearing today is able to heal your yesterday!

Jesus said, "*Woman, thou art loosed.*"

He did not call her by name.

He wasn't speaking to her just as a person.

He spoke to her femininity.

He spoke to the song in her.

He spoke to the lace in her.

As if to a crumbling rose, Jesus spoke to what she could, and would, have been. I believe the Lord spoke to the twinkle that existed in her eye when she was a child; to the girlish glow that makeup can never seem to recapture. He spoke to her God-given uniqueness. He spoke to her gender.

Her problem didn't begin suddenly. It had existed in her life for 18 years. We are looking at a woman who had a personal war going on inside her. These struggles must have tainted many other areas of her life. The infirmity that attacked her life was physical. However, many women also wrestle with infirmities in emotional traumas. These infirmities can be just as challenging as a physical affliction.

YOUR HEALING JOURNEY

Invite the Holy Spirit to come and help you identify your infirmity—the specific areas where God wants to bring healing into your life. Allow Him to speak directly and intimately to you. He always comes with love, compassion, and hope. Trust His process.

Then, ask God to start giving you passages from Scripture to stand on as promises for healing. He doesn't want to leave you simply recognizing your infirmity; He wants to give you hope from His Word that there is a future beyond your past.

LET GOD BE YOUR RESCUER AND HEALER

And, behold, there was a woman which
had a spirit of infirmity eighteen years...
and could in no wise lift up herself.
—LUKE 13:11

The Scriptures plainly show that this infirm woman had tried to lift herself. People who stand on the outside can easily criticize and assume that the infirm woman lacks effort and fortitude. That is not always the case. Some situations in which we can find ourselves defy willpower.

We feel unable to change.

The Scriptures say that she "could in no wise lift up herself." That implies she had employed various means of self-ministry. Isn't it amazing how the same people who lift up countless others often cannot lift themselves?

This type of person may be a tower of faith and prayer for others, but impotent when it comes to her own limitations. That person may be the one others rely upon. Sometimes we esteem others more important than ourselves. We always become the martyr.

It is wonderful to be self-sacrificing, but watch out for self-disdain! If we don't apply some of the medicine that we use on others to strengthen ourselves, our patients will be healed and we will be dying.

YOUR HEALING JOURNEY

As you begin your healing journey, be careful not to fall prey to the temptation of trying to lift yourself—even though you've been able to lift others up successfully. You can't do it, so stop trying.

You may be able to help lift up others during their times of infirmity or seasons of difficulty, but for your own healing and freedom you must completely surrender to the Holy Spirit's work. Let God be your Rescuer and Healer rather than you trying to do this impossible work by yourself.

RECOGNIZE THE SPIRIT OF INFIRMITY

Behold, there was a woman which had a
spirit of infirmity eighteen years....
—LUKE 13:11

Many things can engender disappointment and depression.

In this woman's case, a spirit of infirmity had gripped her life. A spirit can manifest itself in many forms.

For some it may be low self-esteem caused by child abuse, rape, wife abuse, or divorce. I realize that these are natural problems, but they are rooted in spiritual ailments. One of the many damaging things that can affect us today is divorce, particularly for women, who often look forward to a happy relationship.

When you begin to realize that your past does not necessarily dictate the outcome of your future, then you can release the hurt. It is impossible to inhale new air until you exhale the old. I pray that as you continue on this journey,

God would give the grace of releasing where you have been so you can receive what God has for you now.

Exhale, then inhale; there is more for you!

YOUR HEALING JOURNEY

In order to break free from a spirit of infirmity, it is important for you to recognize its influence in your life. Many natural problems have their roots in spiritual ailments. To clearly identify the spiritual strongholds at work in your life, start by praying,

Father God, show me areas in my life that have been directly caused by or are under the influence of a spirit of infirmity.

God wants to heal you from past hurts that are responsible for present bondages. For Him to do so, you must be willing to do some exploration with the Holy Spirit and honestly look for areas that might be afflicted by a spirit of infirmity.

LEARN HOW TO HEAL WELL

And when Jesus saw her, he called her to him....
—LUKE 13:12

Whenever I think on these issues (specifically abuse), I am reminded of what my mother used to say. I was forever coming home with a scratch or cut from schoolyard play. My mother would take the Band-Aid off, clean the wound and say, "Things that are covered don't heal well." Mother was right. Things that are covered do not heal well.

Perhaps Jesus was thinking on this order when He called the infirm woman to come forward. It takes a lot of courage even in church today to receive ministry in sensitive areas. The Lord, though, is the kind of physician who can pour on the healing oil. Uncover your wounds in His presence and allow Him to gently heal the injuries. One woman found healing in the hem of His garment (see Mark 5:25-29). There is a balm in Gilead (see Jer. 8:22)!

Even when the victim survives, there is still a casualty. It is the death of trust. Surely you realize that little girls tend to be trusting and unsuspicious. When those who should nurture and protect them violate that trust through illicit behavior, multiple scars result. It is like programming a computer with false information; you can get out of it only what has been programmed into it.

Your Healing Journey

No matter what you have suffered in the past—shame, abuse, bullying, harsh words—God is able to bring healing and wholeness. As you go through this healing process, do not try to cover up your wounds with a "Band-Aid." This response is common for all people, especially those of faith.

Sometimes, as people of faith, we mistakenly assume that we should pretend away all of our problems rather than boldly acknowledging them and bringing them to the Healer. We put up a spiritual front, all the while dying inside. Be honest with God about your hurt. Your past. Your rejection. Whatever area you need healing in, Jesus can truly and abundantly supply.

One reason that people do not receive inner healing is because they hide information, hoping it will just go away on its own. It won't. Remember, God reveals what He wants to heal!

Day Six

TRANSFORM YOUR FRAME OF REFERENCE

*Do not conform to the pattern of this world, but
be transformed by the renewing of your mind.
Then you will be able to test and approve what
God's will is—his good, pleasing and perfect will.*
—ROMANS 12:2, NIV

We frame our references around our own experiences. If those experiences are distorted, our ability to comprehend spiritual truths can be off-center. I know that may sound very negative for someone who is in that circumstance.

What do you do when you have been poorly programmed by life's events? I've got good news! You can reprogram your mind through the Word of God.

The Greek word *metamorphôô* is translated as "transformed" in the Romans 12:2 text. Literally, it means to change into another form! You can have a complete metamorphosis through the Word of God.

It has been my experience as a pastor, who does extensive counseling in my own ministry and abroad, that many abused people, women in particular, tend to flock to legalistic churches who see God primarily as a disciplinarian. Many times the concept of fatherhood for them is a harsh code of ethics. This type of domineering ministry may appeal to those who are performance-oriented. I understand that morality is important in Christianity; however, there is a great deal of difference between morality and legalism. It is important that God not be misrepresented. He is a balanced God, not an extremist.

> *The Word became flesh and made his dwelling among us. We have seen his glory, the glory of the one and only Son, who came from the Father, full of grace and truth* (John 1:14 NIV).

The glory of God is manifested only when there is a balance between grace and truth. Religion doesn't transform. Legalism doesn't transform. For the person who feels dirty, harsh rules could create a sense of self-righteousness. God doesn't have to punish you to heal you. Jesus has already prayed for you.

> *Sanctify them through thy truth: thy word is truth* (John 17:17).

Jesus simply shared grace and truth with that hurting woman. He said, "Woman, thou art loosed." Believe the Word of God and be free.

. . . .

YOUR HEALING JOURNEY

To experience true healing, one of the first things you need to transform is your mind. Your frame of reference. Your healing will only go as far as your thinking—namely, your thinking about God. God does not need to hurt you to heal you. He doesn't need to punish you to bring you into wholeness.

Legalism is just as dangerous as the infirmity you want to be delivered from. Don't fall into the trap of thinking that you need to check off a list of spiritual "to dos" in order to be qualified to receive healing. Yes, healing is a journey. Of course, there are certain processes you will engage upon this path. At the same time, so many women never even begin their journey because they think in order for God to bring healing and wholeness to their lives, they need to get everything fixed, cleaned up, and perfectly in order to qualify themselves for Heaven's healing salve. This is a lie.

Change your frame of reference. God is not a stern taskmaster or harsh disciplinarian; He is full of love and grace. He accepts you right where you are so He can effectively bring you into where you are destined to go!

BE CAREFUL WHAT YOU ARE RECEIVING

Neither give place to the devil.
—EPHESIANS 4:27

By nature a woman is a receiver. She is not physically designed to be a giver. Her sexual and emotional fulfillment becomes somewhat dependent on the giving of her male counterpart (in regard to intimate relationships). There is a certain vulnerability that is a part of being a receiver. In regard to reproduction (sexual relationships), the man is the contributing factor, and the woman is the receiver.

What is true of the natural is true of the spiritual. Men tend to act out of what they perceive to be facts, while women tend to react out of their emotions. If your actions and moods are not a reaction to the probing of the Holy Spirit, then you are reacting to the subtle taunting of the enemy. He is trying to produce his destructive fruit in your home, heart, and even in your relationships. Receiver, be careful what you receive! Moods and attitudes that satan would offer, you need to resist. Tell the enemy, "This is not me, and I don't receive it." It is his job to offer it and your job to resist it. If you do your job, all will go well.

Submit yourselves, then, to God. Resist the devil, and he will flee from you (James 4:7 NIV).

Don't allow the enemy to plug in to you and violate you through his subtle seductions. He is a giver and he is looking for a receiver. You must discern his influence if you are going to rebuke him. Anything that comes, any mood that is not in agreement with God's Word, is satan trying to plug in to the earthly realm through your life. He wants you to believe you cannot change. He loves prisons and chains! Statements like, "This is just the way I am," or "I am in a terrible mood today," come from lips that accept what they ought to reject.

Never allow yourself to settle for anything less than the attitude God wants you to have in your heart. Don't let satan have your day, your husband, or your home. Eve could have put the devil out!

YOUR HEALING JOURNEY

As a woman, it is your nature to receive. Your enemy, the devil, is very intentional about "giving" certain thought patterns that are purposed to keep you in bondage. He is perpetually making offers. Thoughts of fear, insecurity, inadequacy, guilt, shame, and condemnation. The Bible describes him as one like a roaring lion, seeking those he may devour (see 1 Pet. 5:8). He is looking for those who willing-ly receive his invitations to imprisonment. Don't fall into his trap like Eve did!

Sin did not begin with Eve's action; it began when she embraced and agreed with the lie of the serpent. It began in her mind and in her heart before she extended her hand toward the forbidden fruit. Don't receive the lies of the en-emy. Resist them, standing steadfast in your faith! When he comes with a bombardment against your mind, start to speak out the promises of God—out loud! Declare what the Word of God says about you, as that is your surefire weapon to defeat and extinguish every fiery dart of the enemy.

NURTURE THE WORD OF THE LORD

I have hidden your word in my heart,
that I might not sin against you.
—PSALM 119:11, NLT

It is not enough to reject the enemy's plan. You must nurture the Word of the Lord. You need to draw the promise of God and the vision for the future to your breast. It is a natural law that anything not fed will die. Whatever you have drawn to the breast is what is growing in your life. Breast-feeding holds several advantages for what you feed: (a) it hears your heartbeat; (b) it is warmed by your closeness; (c) it draws nourishment from you. Caution: Be sure you are nurturing what you want to grow and starving what you want to die.

As you read this, you may feel that life is passing you by. You often experience success in one area and gross defeat in others. You need a burning desire for the future, the kind of desire that overcomes past fear and inhibitions. You will remain chained to your past and all the secrets therein until you decide: Enough is enough!

I am telling you that when your desire for the future peaks, you can break out of prison. I challenge you to sit down and write 30 things you would like to do with your life and scratch them off, one by one, as you accomplish them. There is no way you can plan for the future and dwell in the past at the same time.

I feel an earthquake coming into your prison! It is midnight—the turning point of days! It is your time for a change. Praise God and escape out of the dungeons of your past.

YOUR HEALING JOURNEY

The Word of God is what gives you clear vision for your future. Scripture tells us that when we don't have vision, we perish—we die. We become open to believe the lying words of the enemy when we are not filled with the vision-forming words of God. More than physical death, the absence of vision creates stagnancy in our lives. Think about it. It will always be difficult for us to have the resolve to break out of the prison of the past when we don't have a vision for the future. This is why the Word is so important. It gives hope and vision.

Open the Scriptures and ask the Holy Spirit to personalize the Word for you. Ask Him to personalize the promises to give you hope and vision for your future. Don't worry, this is not taking the Bible out of context. It's reading with eyes that see how God's promises, declarations, and announcements are available for you today. Start with passages like Jeremiah 29:11, where God promises to give a hope and a future. Though that timeless promise was originally for God's people in that specific era, the context is everything. They were a people in exile. They were strangers living in a strange land. God was releasing this vision of hope and a future into the midst of a visionless people. All they could see was exile. All they could think about was, "We're not where we should be." Maybe you feel like this. The same God of hope wants to speak words of vision, life, destiny, and future over you, just as He did for His people in the days of Jeremiah.

THE HEALING POWER OF FORGETTING WHAT'S BEHIND

Brethren, I count not myself to have apprehended:
but this one thing I do, forgetting those things
which are behind, and reaching forth unto those
things which are before, I press toward the mark
for the prize of the high calling of God in Christ
Jesus. Let us therefore, as many as be perfect, be
thus minded: and if in any thing ye be otherwise
minded, God shall reveal even this unto you.
—PHILIPPIANS 3:13-15

Have you ever noticed how hard it is to communicate with people who will not give you their attention? Pain will not continue to rehearse itself in the life of a preoccupied, distracted person. Distracted people almost seem weird. They do not respond!

Every woman has something she wishes she could forget. There is a principle to learn here. Forgetting isn't a memory lapse; it is a memory release! Like carbon dioxide the body can no longer use, exhale it and let it go out of your spirit.

Jesus set the infirm woman free. She was able to stand upright. The crippling condition of her infirmity was removed by the God who cares, sees, and calls the infirmity to the dispensary of healing and deliverance. You can call upon Him even in the middle of the night. Like a 24-hour medical center, you can reach Him at any time. He is touched by the feeling of your infirmity.

> *For we have not an high priest which cannot be touched with the feeling of our infirmities; but was in all points tempted like as we are, yet without sin* (Hebrews 4:15).

In the name of our High Priest, Jesus Christ, I curse the infirmity that has bowed the backs of God's women. I pray that, as we share together out of the Word of God, the Holy Spirit would roll you into the recovery room where you can fully realize that the trauma is over. I am excited to say that God never loosed anybody He wasn't going to use mightily. May God reveal healing and purpose as we continue to seek Him.

YOUR HEALING JOURNEY

It's time to exhale your infirmity. Even though the word "distraction" often carries negative connotations, it is certainly not negative when you are too distracted by your destiny to consider your destructive history.

Not all history needs to be healed. Scripture calls us to remember the works of God in our lives and constantly bring to mind how His sovereign fingerprint has been present in our history. This is healthy history. History becomes our enemy when it is laden with trauma—trauma that the enemy wants to use to keep you stuck in the past.

History is your enemy when it keeps you from advancing toward your destiny. When it moves you forward, history is functioning the way God intended. When it is stifling you, it's time to embrace the apostle Paul's perspective. Let go to the past and press toward what lies ahead. Forget what's behind and move toward what's ahead. Forgetting the past can be a great gift when the past is constantly seeking to maintain your imprisonment.

GUARDING YOUR LEGACY
IN YOUR CHILDREN

Lo, children are an heritage of the Lord: and the
fruit of the womb is his reward. As arrows are
in the hand of a mighty man; so are children of
the youth. Happy is the man that hath his quiver
full of them: they shall not be ashamed, but
they shall speak with the enemies in the gate.
—PSALM 127:3-5

Children are living epistles that should stand as evidence to
the future that the past made some level of contribution.

The psalmist David wrote a brief note that is as loud as
an atomic bomb. It speaks to the heart of men about their
attitude toward their offspring. This was David, the man
whose indiscretion with Bathsheba had produced a love
child. Though inappropriately conceived, the baby was loved
nonetheless. David is the man who lay upon the ground in
sackcloth and ashes praying feverishly for mercy as his child
squirmed in the icy hands of death. Somewhere in a tent the

cold silence slowly grew. The squirming stopped, the crying stilled; the baby had gone into eternal rest. If anybody knows the value of children, it is those who just left theirs in the ground. David's son, Solomon, wrote: *"As arrows are in the hand of a mighty man; so are children of the youth."* Perhaps Solomon had heard about his father's grief. He may have pictured the tears his father shed as they lowered his arrow into the ground.

Why did he compare children to arrows? Maybe it was for their potential to be propelled into the future. Perhaps it was for the intrinsic gold mine that lies in the heart of every child who is shot through the womb. Maybe he was trying to tell us that children go where we, their parents, aim them. Could it be that we, as parents, must be responsible enough to place them in the kind of bow that will accelerate their success and emotional well-being? How happy I am to have a quiver full of arrows.

If someone must be hurt, if it ever becomes necessary to bear pains, weather strong winds, or withstand trials or opposition, let it be adults and not children. Whatever happens, happens. I can accept the fate before me. I was my father's arrow and my mother's heart. My father is dead, but his arrows are yet soaring in the wind. You will never know him; he is gone. However, my brother, my sister, and I are flying, soaring, scientific proof that he was, and through us continues to be. So don't worry about me; I am an arrow shot. If I don't succeed, I have had the greatest riches known to man.

I have had an opportunity to test the limits of my destiny. Whether preferred or rejected, let the record show: I am here. Oh, God, let me hit my target! But if I miss and plummet to the ground, then at least I can say, "I have been shot!"

YOUR HEALING JOURNEY

Whether you currently have children or not, it is vital that as a woman you recognize the preciousness of safeguarding the next generation.

Even though you may be on a journey to healing right now, refuse to let the past that imprisoned you have an impact on the next generation. It doesn't have to. In fact, it can end with you. Declare that: "The past ends with me, in Jesus's Name!"

Only pass on the history that will propel the next generation into their destiny and continue your legacy. You don't need to let your legacy be defined by the bondages, faults, and setbacks that plagued you. That's a lie of the enemy. You can break the cycle and watch your children flourish!

MOVED BY COMPASSION

*And Jesus went forth, and saw a great
multitude, and was moved with compassion
toward them, and he healed their sick.*
—MATTHEW 14:14

I earnestly believe that where there is no compassion, there can be no lasting change. As long as Christian leadership secretly jeers and sneers at the perversion that comes into the Church, there will be no healing. Perversion is the offspring of abuse! As long as we crush what is already broken by our own prejudices and phobias, there will be no healing. The enemy robs us of our healing power by robbing us of our concern.

Compassion is the mother of miracles! When the storm had troubled the waters and the disciples thought they would die, they didn't challenge Christ's power; they challenged His compassion. The disciples went into the back of the ship and said, *"Carest thou not that we perish?"* (Mark 4:38). They understood that if there is no real compassion, then there can be no miracle.

Until we, as priests, are touched with the feelings of our parishioners' illnesses rather than just turned off by their symptoms, they will not be healed.

To every husband who wants to see his wife healed, to every mother who has a little girl with a woman's problem—the power to heal is in the power to care.

If you are a broken arrow, please allow someone into the storm. I know you usually do not allow anyone to come to your aid. I realize a breach of trust may have left you leery of everyone, but the walls you built to protect you have also imprisoned you. The Lord wants to loose you out of the dungeon of fear. He does care. We care. No one would take hours away from themselves and from their family praying for you, preaching to you, or even writing this to you if they didn't care.

What happened to the disciples? Jesus rebuked them!

How could they have thought that the God who rode with them in the storm didn't care about the storm? Jesus said, "*Peace, be still*" (Mark 4:39).

To you He is still saying, "Peace, be still!"

YOUR HEALING JOURNEY

Miracles begin as a bent of compassion. Jesus was moved with compassion and healed those who were sick, demonized, and afflicted. Before you receive your healing, receive God's compassion. This strengthens your faith to believe for wholeness as you travel along this journey.

When God is simply a static religious formula that we insert into our spiritual prayer jargon in attempt to secure our desired result, even though we might claim to be "praying in faith," the truth is we are praying in formula.

Faith is not strengthened by knowing the right prayer formula; it's strengthened by being gripped by the compassionate heart of your loving God. When you are convinced that God loves you, is for you, and is moved with compassion to heal your infirmity, you will be strengthened along the journey. No matter what circumstances come your way or how long the perceived delay is, you remain grounded in the steadfast love of God.

You know healing is coming because healing flows out of His unchanging nature as a good God who abounds in compassion!

Day Twelve

COME LIKE A CHILD

And they brought young children to him, that
he should touch them: and his disciples rebuked
those that brought them. But when Jesus saw it,
he was much displeased, and said unto them,
Suffer the little children to come unto me, and
forbid them not: for of such is the kingdom of God.
Verily I say unto you, Whosoever shall not receive
the kingdom of God as a little child, he shall not
enter therein. And he took them up in his arms,
put his hands upon them, and blessed them.
—MARK 10:13-16

It is interesting to me that just before this took place the Lord
was ministering on the subject of divorce and adultery. When
He brought up that subject, someone brought the children to
Him so He could touch them. Broken homes often produce
broken children. These little ones are often caught in the
crossfire of angry parents. It reminds me of a newscast report
on the Gulf War.

It was a listing of the many young men who were accidentally killed by their own military—killed, however innocently, in the confusion of the battle. The newscaster used a term I had not heard before. He called it "friendly fire." I thought, *What is friendly about bleeding to death with your face buried in the hot sun of a strange country? I mean, it doesn't help much when I am dead!* Many children are wounded in the friendly fire of angry parents.

Who were these nameless persons who had the insight and the wisdom to bring the children to the Master? They brought the children to Him that He might touch them. What a strange interruption to a discourse on adultery and divorce. Here are these little children dragging dirty blankets and blank gazes into the presence of a God who is dealing with grown-up problems. He takes time from His busy schedule not so much to counsel them, but just to touch them. That's all it takes. I salute all the wonderful people who work with children. Whether through children's church or public school, you have a very high calling. Don't forget to touch their little lives with a word of hope and a smile of encouragement. It may be the only one some will receive. You are the builders of our future. Be careful, for you may be building a house that we will have to live in!

What was wrong with these disciples that they became angry at some nameless person who aimed these little arrows at the only answer they might ever have gotten to see? Who told them they were too busy to heal their own children?

Jesus stopped teaching on the cause of divorce and marital abuse to touch the victim, to minister to the effect of the abuse. He told them to suffer the little children to come. Suffer the suffering to come! It is hard to work with hurting people, but the time has come for us to suffer the suffering to come. Anything, whether an injured animal or a hospital patient, if it is hurt, is unhappy. We cannot get a wounded lion to jump through hoops! Hurting children as well as hurting adults can carry the unpleasant aroma of bitterness. In spite of the challenge, it is foolish to give up on your own. So they brought the "ouch" to the Band-Aid, and He stopped His message for His mission. Imagine tiny hands outstretched, little faces upturned, perching like sparrows on His knee. They came to get a touch, but He always gives us more than we expected. He held them with His loving arms. He touched with His sensitive hands.

But most of all, He blessed them with His compassionate heart!

YOUR HEALING JOURNEY

What kind of "friendly fire" were you caught in as a child? Teenager? Young adult? Maybe it was your parents' crumbling marriage. Maybe it was something else—another dysfunctional relationship. Perhaps it was a teacher. A boyfriend. A close friend who ended up betraying you.

There are many situations that children are brought into that end up harming them and thus setting them on a certain course for the future.

Become like a child right now and let the Master lay His healing hands upon you. Invite the Holy Spirit into your past and ask Him to shine Heaven's spotlight on broken areas that need wholeness. The goal is not to revisit pain for the purpose of hurting more; it's going to the past root of your present infection.

Often, we try to deal with symptoms by concealing them with a Band-Aid, when really we are placing a cover-up on a growing infection that is festering well below the surface. The Lord shines light on whatever He wants to heal and restore. Trust His process, surrendering in childlike faith.

BECOME LIKE A CHILD

*And said, Verily I say unto you, Except ye be
converted, and become as little children, ye
shall not enter into the kingdom of heaven.*
—MATTHEW 18:3

When Jesus blessed the children, He challenged the adults
to become as children. Oh, to be a child again, to allow
ourselves the kind of relationship with God that we may
have missed as a child. Sometimes we need to allow the Lord
to adjust the damaged places of our past. I am glad to say
that God provides arms that allow grown children to climb
up like children and be nurtured through the tragedies of
early days. Isn't it nice to toddle into the presence of God
and let Him hold you in His arms? In God, we can become
children again.

Salvation is God giving us a chance to start over again. He
will not abuse the children who come to Him.

Through praise, I approach Him like a toddler on
unskillful legs.

In worship, I kiss His face and am held by the caress of His anointing.

He has no ulterior motive, for His caress is safe and wholesome. It is so important that we learn how to worship and adore Him. There is no better way to climb into His arms. Even if you were exposed to grown-up situations when you were a child, God can reverse what you've been through. He'll let the grown-up person experience the joy of being a child in the presence of God!

YOUR HEALING JOURNEY

Become like a child again. Approach God with abandoned worship and exuberant praise! When you received salvation, you were completely converted. You became like a child all over again. Even though your body looked the same, your spirit experienced a total rebirth. Some have given this process a theological title—being "born again."

No matter what you experienced in your personal past or childhood, the Lord Almighty offers you a fresh start. Remember that you are a new creation. What happened yesterday does not need to define today. If you were exposed to grown-up situations as a child, God can supernaturally reverse the trauma that you experienced. You simply need to come before Him as a child—helpless and dependent—and recognize your absolute need for Him.

Sadly, too many adults think they are beyond neediness. This is especially true if we are not experiencing any kind of material or financial lack. The truth is, those of us who believe we are beyond being needy are the neediest of all. We just don't know it. The truth is, a healthy sense of spiritual dependency keeps us vitally connected to the One who provides all things. This includes a fresh start every day, because His mercies are new every morning!

LET GOD'S HEALING WATERS WASH OVER YOUR PAST

You'll forget your troubles; they'll be like old,
faded photographs. Your world will be washed in
sunshine, every shadow dispersed by dayspring.
Full of hope, you'll relax, confident again;
you'll look around, sit back, and take it easy.
Expansive, without a care in the world, you'll
be hunted out by many for your blessing.
—JOB 11:16-19, MSG

It is inconceivable to the injured that the injury can be forgotten. However, as I mentioned earlier in our devotional journey, to forget isn't to develop amnesia. It is to reach a place where the misery is pulled from the memory as a stinger is pulled out of an insect bite.

Once the stinger is gone, healing is inevitable. This passage in Job points out so eloquently that the memory is as *"waters that pass away"* (Job 11:16). Stand in a stream with water around your ankles. The waters that pass by you at that moment you will never see again. So it is with the misery that has challenged your life: Let it go, let it pass away. The brilliance of morning is in sharp contrast to the darkness of night; simply stated, it was night, but now it is day.

Perhaps David understood the aftereffects of traumatic deliverance when he said, *"Weeping may endure for a night, but joy cometh in the morning"* (Ps. 30:5).

YOUR HEALING JOURNEY

Even though it is impossible to develop selective amnesia, completely forgetting the pain that plagued you, it is truly possible for you to stop the flow of the past's poison. The events that happened and facts of your hurt cannot be blotted out from history altogether. However, you can reach into those memories and pull the "stingers" out so that past poison ceases to affect your present progress.

Already on this journey, you have invited the Holy Spirit into your healing process. In doing so, you've most likely had to confront some painful memories. Take this opportunity to soak in the healing waters of God. Relax in His presence. In fact, ask the Lord to let His refreshing waters wash over your past. The hurt. The pain. The rejection. The hidden things you've never told anyone. Even though the waters of His presence cannot remove the past completely, they can bring healing to the pain. They can render the past ineffective at imprisoning you any longer!

THE VOICE OF JESUS'S BLOOD

And to Jesus, the mediator of a new covenant,
and to the sprinkled blood that speaks a
better word than the blood of Abel.
—HEBREWS 12:24, ESV

There is such a security that comes when we are safe in the arms of God. It is when we become secure in our relationship with God that we begin to allow the past to fall from us as a garment. We remember it, but choose not to wear it! I am convinced that resting in the relationship that we have with God heals us from the feelings of vulnerability.

It is a shame that many Christians have not yet rested in the promise of God. Everyone needs reassurance. Little girls as well as grown women need that sense of security. In the process of creating Eve, the mother of all living, His timing was crucial. In fact, God did not unveil her until everything she needed was provided. From establishment to relationship, all things were in order. Innately the woman tends to need stability. She wants no sudden changes that disrupt or compromise her security.

She was meant to be covered, and originally Adam was her covering, to nurture and protect her. My sister, you were made to be covered even as a child. If someone "uncovered" you, there is a feeling of being violated. Even when these feelings are suppressed, and they often are, they are still powerful.

Do you realize that one of the things the blood of Jesus Christ does is cover us? Like Noah's sons who covered their father's nakedness, the blood of Jesus will cover the uncovered. He will not allow you to spend the rest of your life exposed and violated.

YOUR HEALING JOURNEY

Your safety and peace are found in this profound reality—the blood of Jesus covers every area of your life. This includes your past. This includes your failures. This includes your shame. This includes your guilt. This includes your sin. This includes your mistakes. This includes the atrocities that were committed by you or against you. Doesn't matter what it is, nothing is beyond the covering of Jesus's precious blood. Why? Because it goes to the most fundamental root issue—sin.

Jesus's blood is the only covering that internally disinfects. While we cannot "cover up" our pain with proverbial Band-Aids—projecting everything is okay while it's really dying inside—the blood of Jesus is the supernatural covering that goes straight to the root issue of all dysfunction and speaks a better word over you. No matter what voices are bringing accusation and condemnation against you, trying to rename you based on your sins, mistakes, or tragedies, the blood of Jesus is louder. It cries out "Redeemed!" "Reconciled!" "Healed and whole!" "Ransomed!" "Beloved!" "Child of God!" "Treasured Daughter!" Choose to believe the voice of the eternal blood more than the fading cry of a defeated enemy!

THE LORD WATCHES OVER YOU

Then I passed by and saw you kicking about in your blood, and as you lay there in your blood I said to you, "Live!" I made you grow like a plant of the field. You grew and developed and entered puberty. Your breasts had formed and your hair had grown, yet you were stark naked. Later I passed by, and when I looked at you and saw that you were old enough for love, I spread the corner of my garment over you and covered your naked body. I gave you my solemn oath and entered into a covenant with you, declares the Sovereign Lord, and you became mine. I bathed you with water and washed the blood from you and put ointments on you. I clothed you with an embroidered dress and put sandals of fine leather on you. I dressed you in fine linen and covered you with costly garments.
—EZEKIEL 16:6-10, NIV

In Ezekiel, the Lord speaks a message to the nation of Israel with an illustration of an abused woman. He speaks about how, as a child, this little girl was not cared for properly. But the Lord passed by her and salted, swaddled, and cared for her as a baby. He says the baby would have bled to death if He hadn't stopped the bleeding. Did you know that God can stop the bleeding of an abused child?

Even as you grow older, He still watches out for you! He will cover your nakedness.

Reach out and embrace the fact that God has been watching over you all of your life. My sister, He covers you, He clothes you, and He blesses you! Rejoice in Him in spite of the broken places. God's grace is sufficient for your needs and your scars. He will anoint you with oil. The anointing of the Lord be upon you now! May it bathe, heal, and strengthen you as never before.

For the hurting, God has intensive care. There will be a time in your life when God nurtures you through crisis situations. You may not even realize how many times God has intervened to relieve the tensions and stresses of day-to-day living. Every now and then He does us a favor. Yes, a favor, something we didn't earn or can't even explain, except as the loving hand of God. He knows when the load is overwhelming. Many times He moves (it seems to us) just in the nick of time.

The Bible instructs the men to dwell with women according to knowledge (see 1 Pet. 3:7). It will pay every husband to understand that many, many women do not deal easily with such stress as unpaid bills and financial disorder. A feeling of security is a plus, especially in reference to the home.

That same principle is important when it comes to your relationship with God. He is constantly reassuring us that we might have a consolation and a hope for the soul, the mind, and the emotions—steadfast and unmovable. He gives us security and assurance.

YOUR HEALING JOURNEY

From your childhood, the Lord has watched over you. Even before you knew Him, He knew you—and loved you just the same.

God hurts over your hurt. As bad as your pain was, you are still here. You are reading these words right now. The Lord safeguarded your life because He has a divine assignment for you. The crisis that you almost drowned in is going to become the very testimony that pays the devil back for every torment he ever caused you. The waters that should have consumed you are going to become a river of refreshing. How does this happen? When you testify to your deliverance. When your healing becomes your story, and your story becomes the topic of your conversation.

I'm sure in the past, your topic of conversation was your trial. Your tragedy. Your hurt. Your pain. God wants to turn that around. He wants to rewrite and ignite your story. No, He is not going to blot out your history; He's going to do what He's best at—redeeming it. He will rewrite it through healing and He will ignite it as you begin to speak it out.

Your history of redemption will become an invitation calling out to those who are in similar pits and prisons. It will release hope to women who were exactly where you were. Overwhelmed. Drowning. Dying. Hopeless. Your story of healing will challenge every prison door by introducing new possibilities. It is possible to be healed. It is possible to be whole. And it is possible to be loosed!

DO NOT BE AFRAID!

*Also thou shalt lie down, and none
shall make thee afraid.*
—JOB 11:19

This is the word of God to you. God wants to bring you to a place of rest, where there is no pacing the floor, no glaring through frightened eyes at those with whom you are involved. Like a frightened animal backed into a corner, we can become fearful and angry because we don't feel safe.

Christ says, "Woman, thou art loosed!"

There is no torment like inner torment. How can you run from yourself? No matter what you achieve in life, if the clanging, rattling chains of old ghosts are not laid to rest, you will not have any real sense of peace and inner joy.

God says, "None shall make thee afraid." A perfect love casts out fear (see 1 John 4:18)! It is a miserable feeling to spend your life in fear. Many grown women live in a fear that resulted from broken arrow experiences of childhood. This kind of fear can manifest itself in jealousy, depression, and many other distresses.

As you allow the past to pass over you as waters moving in the sea, you will begin to live and rest in a new assurance. God loves you so much that He is even concerned about your rest. Take authority over every flashback and every dream that keeps you linked to the past. Even as we share together here, the peace of God will do a new thing in your life.

YOUR HEALING JOURNEY

Use this moment to take authority over the pain of your past. Don't let what happened keep you in a place of fear anymore. We know that yesterday still has a stronghold over today when we are still tormented and haunted by past events. Even though you are in the present and the past is over, the past still maintains a stronghold as long as you continue to welcome its influence.

Decide today that enough is enough. Break your agreement with the past! Even though you cannot make the past disappear, you can break its hold over your life. Whether you feel anything change or not, declare out loud,

Father, I break my agreement with the past in Jesus's Name!

Right now, I ask for the cleansing blood of Jesus to cover every area of my life that is still under the tormenting influence of what has already happened.

I declare that the past is over and today is a new day!

I declare that my rest is peaceful and my sleep is sound!

I declare that my thoughts are without fear and anxiety!

I declare that my healthy relationships today are not hindered by unhealthy relationships of the past.

Thank You, Jesus, for setting me free!

STOP TRYING TO EARN YOUR DELIVERANCE

*For all have sinned, and come
short of the glory of God.*
—ROMANS 3:23

We were all born in sin and shaped in iniquity. We have no true badge of righteousness that we can wear on the outside. God concluded all are in sin so He might save us from ourselves (see Gal. 3:22). It wasn't the act of sin but the state of sin that brought us into condemnation. We were born in sin, equally and individually shaped in iniquity, and not one race or sociological group has escaped the fact that we are Adam's sinful heritage.

No one person needs any more of the blood of Jesus than any other. Jesus died once and for all. Humanity must come to God on equal terms, each individual totally helpless to earn his or her way to Him. When we come to Him with this attitude, He raises us up by the blood of Christ. He doesn't raise us up because we do good things. He raises us up because we have faith in the finished work on the Cross.

Many in the Church are striving for holiness. What we are striving to perfect has already fallen and will only be restored at the second coming of the Lord. We are often trying to perfect flesh. Flesh is in enmity against God, whether we paint it or not.

What is holiness? To understand it, we must first separate the pseudo from the genuine because when you come into a church it is possible to walk away feeling like a second-class citizen. Many start going overboard trying to be a super-spiritual person in order to compensate for an embarrassing past.

You can't earn deliverance. You have to just receive it by faith. Christ is the only righteousness that God will accept. If outward sanctity had impressed God, Christ would have endorsed the Pharisees.

YOUR HEALING JOURNEY

Every single person who has ever been born—and who will be born in the future—is on level ground when they enter into the world. All are born into sin. This is our heritage dating back to the first sin and the first sinners—Adam and Eve. While this information might not sound very positive, the encouraging truth is that no matter how good you've been (or bad you've been, for that matter), you are unable to earn deliverance. Earning will not position you for breakthrough; only faith will!

So many women are stuck in the rut of spiritual performance. They might think it's holiness, when really it's legalism. They might think they are pursuing godly character, when in fact they are trapped in the bondage of perfectionism. They project a spiritual exterior, but underneath they are desperate for the freedom that only the Liberator can bring. Jesus wants to see you free. He wants to loose you. He wants you healed and whole. To receive this breakthrough, however, you must be willing to participate.

Start by coming clean. Come boldly and honestly to the throne of grace—faults, sins, and all—and recognize your absolute need of Jesus's supernatural power of deliverance. That is your prerequisite for freedom. Not perfection, but rather desperation and utter dependence upon God and God alone.

> *Now that we know what we have—Jesus, this great High Priest with ready access to God—let's not let it slip through our fingers. We don't have a priest who is out of touch with our reality. He's been through weakness and testing, experienced it all—all but the sin. So let's walk right up to him and get what he is so ready to give. Take the mercy, accept the help* (Hebrews 4:14-16 MSG).

SANCTIFIED...FROM THE INSIDE OUT

But if we walk in the light, as he is in the light,
we have fellowship with one another, and the
blood of Jesus, his Son, purifies us from all sin.
—1 JOHN 1:7, NIV

There is a sanctity of your spirit that comes through the blood of the Lord Jesus Christ and sanctifies the innermost part of your being. Certainly, once you get cleaned up in your spirit, it will be reflected in your character and conduct.

You won't be like Mary the mother of Jesus and dress like Mary Magdalene did before she met the Master. The Spirit of the Lord will give you boundaries. On the other hand, people must be loosed from the chains of guilt and condemnation. Many women in particular have been bound by manipulative messages that specialize in control and dominance.

The Church must open its doors and allow people who have a past to enter in. What often happens is they're spending years in the back pew trying to pay through obeisance for something in the past. Congregations often are unwilling to release reformed women. Remember, the same blood that cleanses the man can restore the woman also.

The Bible never camouflaged the weaknesses of the people God used. God used David. God used Abraham. We must divorce our embarrassment about wounded people. Yes, we've got wounded people. Yes, we've got hurting people. Sometimes they break the boundaries and they become lascivious and out of control and we have to readmit them into the hospital and allow them to be treated again. That's what the Church is designed to do. The Church is a hospital for wounded souls.

The staff in a hospital understand that periodically people get sick and they need a place to recover. Now, I'm not condoning the sin. I'm just explaining that it's a reality. Many of the people in Scripture were unholy. The only holy man out of all of the characters in the Bible is Jesus Christ, the righteousness of God.

YOUR HEALING JOURNEY

God did not call the righteous—He called the unrighteous! The reason is that there are no righteous people on the planet. The only Perfect One was and is Jesus Christ.

Sanctification is an inside job. Many people focus on external appearances when it comes to holiness. All this does is produce a culture of condemnation. People end up feeling excluded from the household of faith because they don't look or dress the part. We must be inclusive. We must recognize our mission to be a hospital for the broken.

At the same time, once we receive the saving work of Jesus, the Sanctifier comes to live inside of us. This is the Holy Spirit. He is the One who begins to lead us in the life-giving ways of the Lord. At the day's end, commandments and boundaries are not for our restriction. To think of them this way is to have a wrong view of God.

The Savior who set you free is not looking to bring you back into bondage. This is why the Holy Spirit gives us life-giving, life-enhancing instructions. He will tell us who to build close friendships with. He will confirm if someone is a fit spouse for us. He will lead us in what to say, how to say it, what to think, how to dress, etc. It's a step-by-step process, though. Notice He doesn't overwhelm us all at once, giving us a long list of every area that needs transformation. He is faithful to meet us right where we are and bring us progressively into new levels of godly living.

Remember, the Holy Spirit's commandments are for our benefit, our protection, and our blessing!

Day Twenty

HEAR THE SAVIOR CALLING YOU

*He (Jesus) told them, "Healthy people
don't need a doctor—sick people do."*
—MARK 2:17, NLT

Jesus's actions were massively different from ours. He focused on hurting people. Every time He saw a hurting person, He reached out and ministered to their need. Once when He was preaching, He looked through the crowd and saw a man with a withered hand. He immediately healed him (see Mark 3:1-5). He sat with the prostitutes and the winebibbers, not the upper echelon of His community. Jesus surrounded Himself with broken, bleeding, dirty people. He called a woman who was crippled and bent over (see Luke 13:11-13). She had come to church and sat in the synagogue for years and years and nobody had helped that woman until Jesus saw her. He called her to the forefront.

At first when I thought about His calling her, I thought, *How rude to call her.* Why didn't He speak the word and heal her in her seat? Perhaps God wants to see us moving toward

Him. We need to invest in our own deliverance. We will bring a testimony out of a test. I also believe that someone else there had problems. When we can see someone else overcoming a handicap, it helps us to overcome.

We can't know how long it took her to get up to the front. Handicapped people don't move as fast as others do. We often don't grow as fast as other people grow if we've been suffering for a long time. We are incapacitated. Often what is simple for one person is extremely difficult for another. Jesus challenged this woman's limitations. He called her anyway.

Thank God He calls women with a past. He reaches out and says, "Get up! You can come to Me." Regardless of what a person has done or what kind of abuse one has suffered, He still calls. We may think our secret is worse than anyone else's. Rest assured that He knows all about it, and still draws us with an immutable call.

YOUR HEALING JOURNEY

Jesus came to seek and save the lost. One of the most important things we can do to position ourselves to receive healing, deliverance, and ultimately salvation is recognize our need. It's true that God, in His sovereign power, can do anything. At the same time, there are factors that actually limit or restrict the flow of God's healing power. One such factor is perceived wellness.

If you are dying, but are thoroughly convinced that you are well, most likely you are going to function at the level of your thought process. In other words, your mind—as strong as it is—convinces you that you are something you are not (well), even though you are sick, dying, and in dire need of medical attention.

The same is often true of us—especially in the religious church world. There are so many people who project wellness and health when, in fact, they are dying inside. The very thing that will position them for the Master to see them, take notice of their condition, and call them out, just like the infirm woman in Luke 13, is their infirmity. Their sickness. Their condition. Their bondage. Their prison. The thing they are most ashamed of. The thing that reveals their true condition and state. The ugly reality.

God wants us to bring it before Him, not so He can shame us by projecting it on the iMAX theater screens of Heaven, but so He can be our Great Physician. The Savior is calling. The Healer is extending His hand to you. Don't let pride prevent you from reaching back and receiving your breakthrough!

Day Twenty-One

GOD IS CALLING YOU IN SPITE OF YOUR PAST

*Come unto me, all ye that labour and are
heavy laden, and I will give you rest.*
—MATTHEW 11:28

No matter how difficult life seems, people with a past need to make their way to Jesus. Regardless of the obstacles within and without, they must reach Him. You may have a baby out of wedlock cradled in your arms, but keep pressing on. You may have been abused and molested and never able to talk to anyone about it, but don't cease reaching out for Him. You don't have to tell everyone your entire history. Just know that He calls, on purpose, women with a past. He knows your history, but He called you anyway.

God will give you a miracle. He'll do it powerfully and publicly. Many will say, "Is this the same woman who was bent over and wounded in the church?" Perhaps some will think, *Is this the same woman who had one foot in the church and the other in an affair?*

Many of the people who were a part of the ministry of Jesus's earthly life were people with colorful pasts. Some had indeed always looked for the Messiah to come. Others were involved in things that were immoral and inappropriate.

A good example is Matthew. He was a man who worked in an extremely distasteful profession. He was a tax collector. Few people like tax collectors still today. Their reputation was even worse at that time in history. Matthew collected taxes for the Roman Empire. He had to have been considered a traitor by those who were faithful Jews. Romans were their oppressors. How could he have forsaken his heritage and joined the Romans?

Tax collectors did more than simply receive taxes for the benefit of the government. They were frequently little better than common extortioners. They had to collect a certain amount for Rome, but anything they could collect above that set figure was considered the collector's commission. Therefore they frequently claimed excessive taxes. Often they acted like common thieves.

Regardless of his past, Jesus called Matthew to be a disciple. Later he served as a great apostle and wrote one of the books of the New Testament. Much of the history and greatness of Jesus would be lost to us were it not for Jesus calling Matthew, a man with a past. We must maintain a strong line of demarcation between a person's past and present.

These were the people Jesus wanted to reach. He was criticized for being around questionable characters. Everywhere

He went the oppressed and the rejected followed Him. They knew that He offered mercy and forgiveness.

People with a past have always been able to come to Jesus. He makes them into something wonderful and marvelous. It is said that Mary Magdalene was a prostitute. Christ was moved with compassion for even this base kind of human existence. He never used a prostitute for sex, but He certainly loved them into the Kingdom of God.

YOUR HEALING JOURNEY

Your history does not determine your destiny. If this was the case, Jesus would have very few followers. And even those followers who didn't have a very obvious, blatant past had their own sins and struggles they dealt with. None is qualified to be called or used by the Savior. That is the Good News of the Gospel, illustrated time after time in the Scriptures. Jesus called those whose history had written them off. How about you? Are there specific things in your history that have made you feel unfit to be used by God? Unfit for a hope and a future? Unfit for a life of purpose, meaning, significance, and impact? If so, remember the constant invitation of Jesus: *Come follow Me!*

The Lord is not looking for an excuse from you as to why you are unworthy or unfit to be called. He's God. If He deemed you unfit, He would not be calling. The truth is, He is always calling. The one thing that keeps many people from answering the call is their bondage to the lie that they are not worthy to be called. Believe you are worthy to be called and used by God, not because of your own merit. Surely not! You are well acquainted with your past. But guess what? He knows your past too. Every inch. Every nook and every cranny. Everything is openly exposed before the Lord of all creation. Nothing is hidden from His sight. Should this cause us to shudder? Many think so. At the same time, remember this staggering truth and be encouraged—the One who knows all things is still lovingly inviting you to join Him.

WHAT HAPPENS WHEN YOU'RE FOUND OUT!

And the scribes and Pharisees brought unto him
a woman taken in adultery; and when they had
set her in the midst, they say unto him, Master,
this woman was taken in adultery, in the very act.
Now Moses in the law commanded us, that such
should be stoned: but what sayest thou? This they
said, tempting him, that they might have to accuse
him. But Jesus stooped down, and with his finger
wrote on the ground, as though he heard them not.
So when they continued asking him, he lifted up
himself, and said unto them, He that is without
sin among you, let him first cast a stone at her.

—JOHN 8:3-7

When Christ was teaching in the temple courts, there were those who tried to trap Him in His words. They knew that His ministry appealed to the masses of lowly people. They thought that if they could get Him to say some condemning things, the people wouldn't follow Him anymore.

Clearly Jesus saw the foolish religious pride in their hearts. He was not condoning the sin of adultery. He simply understood the need to meet people where they were and minister to their need. He saw the pride in the Pharisees and ministered correction to that pride. He saw the wounded woman and ministered forgiveness. Justice demanded that she be stoned to death. Mercy threw the case out of court.

Have you ever wondered where the man was who had been committing adultery with this woman? She had been caught in the very act. Surely they knew who the man was. There still seems to be a double standard today when it comes to sexual sin. Often we look down on a woman because of her past but overlook who she is now.

Jesus, however, knew the power of a second chance.

YOUR HEALING JOURNEY

Whatever your past history or your present struggle, Jesus wants to give you a second chance. Perhaps you think you've exhausted His grace. Impossible! His grace is endless. It reaches as far as His love, and His love endures forever.

Of course, grace is not license to exploit the love of God. "God loves me so I can live however and do whatever I want." Are there people who embrace this false perspective? Sadly, yes. Such a perspective reveals that the person needs a greater revelation of how extravagant God's grace truly is. In view of His grace, we are called up higher.

Just like the woman caught in adultery, all of us—at one point or another—come to this place where we feel "caught" in our sin. No matter how much we try to hide it or conceal it, it finds us out. We can live in the darkness for only so long before what's in the dark comes into the light.

How does Jesus respond when you get "found out" and your sin comes to light? Consider this woman who was found out. While religion wanted to stone her, Jesus leveled the playing field reminding everyone present that they equally deserved the same stones of punishment for the sins they committed. He radically forgave her of her sin and radically empowered her to move beyond her sin. This same Jesus offers radical grace and divine empowerment for your life today!

THE POWER OF A SECOND CHANCE

When Jesus had lifted up himself, and saw none but the woman, he said unto her, Woman, where are those thine accusers? hath no man condemned thee? She said, No man, Lord. And Jesus said unto her, Neither do I condemn thee: go, and sin no more.
—JOHN 8:10-11

There are those today who are very much like this woman. They have come into the Church. Perhaps they have made strong commitments to Christ and have the very Spirit of God living within them. Yet they walk as cripples. They have been stoned and ridiculed. They may not be physically broken and bowed over, but they are wounded within. Somehow the Church must find room to throw off condemnation and give life and healing.

The blood of Jesus is efficacious, cleansing the woman who feels unclean. How can we reject what He has cleansed and made whole? Just as He said to the woman then, He proclaims today, "Neither do I condemn thee: go and sin no more." How can the Church do any less?

The chains that bind are often from events that we have no control over. The woman who is abused is not responsible for the horrible events that happened in her past. Other times the chains are there because we have willfully lived lives that bring bondage and pain.

Regardless of the source, Jesus comes to set us free. He is unleashing the women of His Church. He forgives, heals, and restores. Women can find the potential of their future because of His wonderful power operating in their lives.

YOUR HEALING JOURNEY

Jesus comes to forgive your past and give you hope for a future. Consider it for a moment—you cannot move toward your future, your purpose, and your destiny with any sense of confidence if you are still plagued by the past. Jesus wants to give you a second chance! And if you feel like you've already wasted such a chance, take heart—this is the God whose forgiveness is infinite.

Sometimes we have control over past events; sometimes we don't. Whatever the source of pain, shame, or brokenness, we need to make ourselves completely vulnerable to the Healer. This is where it is important to consider Jesus's example in John 8. This woman was truly vulnerable before Jesus. Surely she felt dirty, there on the ground, before Perfection Incarnate. The only One who had any right to cast a stone in her direction forgave her. He extended mercy. And a step further, He released grace for her to "go and sin no more." Mercy held back the stones that she deserved, while grace called her to live beyond her lifestyle of sin. That's not where a daughter of God belongs, and that's not where you belong.

Jesus did not condemn her; He empowered her. Receive His words of empowerment over you today. If He tells you to go and "sin no more," He is not expecting absolute perfection. Rather, He is letting you know that life outside of your prison is possible!

Day Twenty-Four

YOUR INTERCESSOR
AND ADVOCATE

*Therefore he is able, once and forever, to save
those who come to God through him. He lives
forever to intercede with God on their behalf.*
—HEBREWS 7:25, NLT

The enemy is planning and plotting your destruction. He
has watched you with wanton eyes. He has great passion and
perseverance. Jesus told Peter, "*Satan hath desired to have you,
that he may sift you as wheat: but I have prayed for thee*" (Luke
22:31-32). Satan lusts after God's children. He wants you.
He craves for you with an animalistic passion. He awaits an
opportunity for attack. In addition, he loves to use people to
fulfill the same kinds of lust upon one another.

Desire is a motivating force. It can make you do things
you never thought yourself capable of doing. Lust can make
a man break his commitment to himself. It will cause people
to reach after things they never thought they would reach for.

Like Peter, you may have gone through some horrible times, but Jesus intercedes on your behalf. No matter the struggles women have faced, confidence is found in the ministry of our High Priest. He prays for you. Faith comes when you recognize that you can't help yourself. Only trust in Christ can bring you through. Many have suffered mightily, but Christ gives the strength to overcome the attacks of satan and human, selfish lust.

YOUR HEALING JOURNEY

You have an enemy who rages in anger against you. Why? He is well aware of the divine solutions you carry that dismantle his strategies.

As a daughter of God, you are a divine solution. In the Garden of Eden, after God created Adam, He deemed that it was "not good" for man to be alone. There was a problem in perfection. There was a missing link in absolute paradise. This is what caused Him to create Eve.

Consider your unique identity for a moment, as a woman. We often look back to Eden as the blueprint for perfection. While this is absolutely true, God saw lack in the midst of perfection. He observed something missing—a problem that required a divine solution. This is why He created woman, and this is why the hosts of hell rage against you. You, as a woman, offer solutions to the earth that no one else can.

Don't dismiss the enemy's attacks as random or happenstance. Though he rages against you, be encouraged—you have a Great Intercessor who lives forever to pray for you. His Name is Jesus!

JUST LET IT GO!

A thief is only there to steal and kill and destroy.
I came so they can have real and eternal life,
more and better life than they ever dreamed of.
—JOHN 10:10, MSG

One of the things that makes many women particularly vulnerable to different types of abuse and manipulation is their maternal instinct. Wicked men frequently capitalize on this tendency in order to have their way with women. Mothers like to take care of little helpless babies. It seems that the more helpless a man acts, the more maternal you become. Women instinctively are nurturers, reaching out to needy people in order to nurture, love, and provide inner strength. All too often, these healthy desires are taken advantage of by those who would fulfill their own lusts. The gift of discernment must operate in your life.

The number of cases of violence within relationships and marriages is growing at an alarming rate. The incidence of date rape is reaching epidemic proportions. The fastest growing form of murder today is within relationships. Husbands and wives and girlfriends and boyfriends are killing one another. Often women have taken to murder in order to escape the constant violence of an abusive husband.

Another form of abuse is more subtle. There are men who often coerce women into a sexual relationship by claiming that they love them. Deception is emotional rape! It is a terrible feeling to be used by someone. Looking for love in all the wrong places leads to a feeling of abuse. A deceiver may continually promise that he will leave his wife for his lover. This woman holds on to that hope, but it never seems to come true. He makes every kind of excuse possible for taking advantage of her, and she, because of her vulnerability, follows blindly along until the relationship has gone so far that she is trapped.

Men who have sex with women without being committed to them are just as guilty of abuse as a rapist. A woman may have given her body to such a man, but she did so because of certain expectations. When someone uses another person for sex by misleading them, it is the same as physical rape. The abuse is more subtle, but it amounts to the same thing. Both the abuser and the victim are riding into a blazing inferno. Anything can happen when a victim has had enough.

Some women suffer from low self-esteem. They are victims and they don't even know it. Perhaps every time something goes wrong, you think it's your fault. It is not your fault if you are being abused in this way; it is your fault if you don't allow God's Word to arrest sin and weakness in your life. It is time to let go of every ungodly relationship. Do it now!

YOUR HEALING JOURNEY

This is a very confrontational entry, but one that is very much needed. This is not simply a matter of "don't do this" when it comes to dating. That would be a very shallow way for us to examine this sensitive subject. Rather, you need to be rooted and grounded in your identity. When you know who you truly are, you know what you will not settle for.

Sadly, past pain—when not brought to the Healer and dealt with appropriately—can create a victim identity that positions you to embrace destructive, exploitive relationships. Anything just to feel "wanted." To feel special. To feel like someone notices you. You don't notice yourself, so you need someone else to do it. You don't value yourself, so you are willing to accept anything from anyone to give you the feeling of being valued—even if it's a cheap counterfeit. Let it go—you're worth more than that!

You are valuable beyond comprehension. Don't allow yourself to be taken advantage of by those who claim to love you when they are simply wanting to use you to satisfy lustful desires. That is not love, nor is it an expression of value. Not by a long shot. You are better than that. Remember your identity as God's divine solution! Don't let the hurts, pain, abuse, or shame of your past dictate your today. The past is over. Even as you are healing from it and receiving deliverance, you can still refuse to embrace "relationships" that are trying to treat you like you thought you deserved to be treated. What you thought was wrong! Just let it go, move on, and embrace what God says about who you are. This is foundational in your healing process.

THE LORD IS YOUR HUSBAND AND MAKER

*For your Maker is your husband—the Lord
Almighty is his name—the Holy One of Israel is
your Redeemer; he is called the God of all the earth.*
—ISAIAH 54:5, NIV

Some have been abused, misused, and victimized. Some played a part in their own demise. There are people who live in fear and pain because of the immoral relationships that took place in the home. If you know this kind of pain, the Lord wants to heal you. Those who have a desperate need for male attention have usually come from a situation where there has been an absence of positive male role models in the home. Perhaps you didn't get enough nurturing as a girl. Therefore, it becomes easy to compromise and do anything to find male acceptance and love.

The Lord is calling the hurting to Him. He will fill that void in your life. He wants to be that heavenly Father who will mend your heart with a positive role model. Through the Spirit, He wants to hold and nurture you. Millions have longed for a positive hug and nurturing embrace from fathers without ever receiving what they longed for. There is a way to fill that emptiness inside. It is through a relationship with God.

There is a place in the heart of most women for an intimate and yet platonic relationship. Big brothers tend to protect their little sisters. They tend to watch for traps that may be placed in the sisters' way. Abused women have confused ideas about relationships and may not understand a healthy platonic relationship with the opposite sex. This confusion comes from the past. One lady said that she could never trust a man who didn't sleep with her. Actually, she had a long history of victimization that led to her poor view of relationships.

Society often places a woman's worth on her sexual appeal. Nothing is further from the truth. Self-esteem cannot be earned by performance in bed. Society suggests that the only thing men want is sex. Although the male sex drive is very strong, all men are not like Amnon, the rapist (see 2 Sam. 13). Men, in general, are not the enemy. We cannot use Amnon as a basis to evaluate all men. Do not allow an Amnon experience to taint your future.

Draw a line of demarcation and say to yourself, "That was then and this is now!"

YOUR HEALING JOURNEY

Don't seek out a man to determine your worth. This is a snare for so many women, as a godless society is constantly calling for women to be identified by how men sexually respond to them. Know this: Your value is not rooted in your sexual appeal, and your self-esteem cannot be earned by performance in bed.

Remember the words from Scripture that the Lord, the Maker of Heaven and Earth, is your husband. No man or person can speak so definitively about who you are. They don't know you like God does. He knit you together in your mother's womb. He knew you before you knew you. If anyone has any authority to speak worth, value, and self-esteem over you, it's God and God alone. Be encouraged by the positive things people say. Be challenged by the legitimate criticism they offer. But at day's end, only be defined by God's definition of you.

No human being can speak words that impact you and define your life like the words that proceed from the mouth of God.

Day Twenty-Seven

GOD'S INTENSIVE CARE UNIT

He that dwelleth in the secret place of the most High
shall abide under the shadow of the Almighty.
—PSALM 91:1

The Song of Solomon shows a progression of the relationship between the author and his wife. First she was his sister, then she became his bride. He also wrote of protecting a little sister. There are many new converts in the Church who are to be treated as little sisters. Solomon says, *"inclose her with boards of cedar"* (Song of Sol. 8:9). The Church is God's cedar chest!

God's people are to nurture and protect one another. It makes no difference how tempestuous our past life has been. Even in the face of abuse, God still cares.

Did you know that God has intensive care? He will take you in His arms. That love of God is flowing into broken lives all over the country. Don't believe for one moment that no one cares; God cares and the Church is learning to become a conduit of that concern. At last, we are in the school of love.

Jesus said, "*By this shall all men know that ye are my disciples, if ye have love one to another*" (John 13:35).

YOUR HEALING JOURNEY

Jesus is raising up His Church as a haven of safety and sanctuary for healing in this time. This was always the divine design for the community of God on the earth. The problem is that, over the years, religion has often replaced the responsibility to love and care for the hurting.

Don't let your negative history with the Church or religion disfigure your view of God's divine remedy. The purpose of His called-out community—the Church—is not to look pious and religious; they are called out to extend the healing hands of Jesus to the suffering.

The Church should be a shade tree for you during this time of healing. Again, don't let your past experiences define your present pursuit of God. He wants to heal you everywhere that you hurt.

Day Twenty-Eight

OPEN UP AND RECEIVE YOUR HEALING

*Bear ye one another's burdens, and
so fulfill the law of Christ.*
—GALATIANS 6:2

Love embraces the totality of the other person. It is impossible to completely and effectively love someone without being included in that other person's history. Our history has made us who we are. The images, scars, and victories that we live with have shaped us into the people we have become. We will never know who a person is until we understand where they have been.

The secret of being transformed from a vulnerable victim to a victorious, loving person is found in the ability to open your past to someone responsible enough to share your weaknesses and pains. You don't have to keep reliving it. You can release it.

There can be no better first step toward deliverance than to find a Christian counselor or pastor and come out of hiding.

Of course, some care should be taken. No one is expected to air their personal life to everyone or even everywhere. However, if you seek God's guidance and the help of confident leadership, you will find someone who can help you work through the pain and suffering of being a victim. The Church is a body. No one operates independent of another. We are all in this walk together, and therefore can build one another up and carry some of the load with which our sisters are burdened.

There is hope for victims. There is no need to feel weak when one has Jesus Christ. His power is enough to bring about the kinds of changes that will set you free. He is calling, through the work of the Holy Spirit, for you to be set free.

YOUR HEALING JOURNEY

As you share your journey to healing and freedom with others, you are actually participating in the healing process. It's not simply sharing about your struggle; as you find someone who you trust to share your journey with, you are doing what James wrote about: *"Make this your common practice: Confess your sins to each other and pray for each other so that you can live together whole and healed"* (James 5:16 MSG).

Pray and ask God to send you the right person or group. Ask Him to lead you to the wise and compassionate voice of counsel. Do not enter into this kind of accountability relationship flippantly. This process is absolutely integral when it comes to you receiving the healing that you long for. When we keep our struggle in the dark, it festers. It eats away at us. The truth is, we cannot conquer it alone. We need iron to sharpen us. We need those who speak as oracles of God, releasing words of life, hope, healing, and purpose over us. To seek perfection, you are setting yourself up for instant disappointment. No person, friend, or counselor will be perfect. Only the Wonderful Counselor fits that description. At the same time, the Wonderful Counselor speaks to others in unique ways through the Holy Spirit. The very words of life and healing that you need might just be in the voice of another. Recognize this. Open up. Ask the Lord for guidance to find the right people. And trust His process!

YOU ARE NOT CONDEMNED

*There is therefore now no condemnation to
them which are in Christ Jesus, who walk
not after the flesh, but after the Spirit.*
—ROMANS 8:1

Have you ever had anything happen to you that changed you forever? Somehow, you were like a palm tree and you survived. Yet you knew you would never be the same. Perhaps you have spent every day since then bowed over. You could in no wise lift up yourself. You shout. You sing. You skip. But when no one is looking, when the crowd is gone and the lights are out, you are still that trembling, crying, bleeding mass of pain that is abused, bowed, bent backward, and crippled.

Maybe you are in the church, but you are in trouble. People move all around you, and you laugh, even entertain them. You are fun to be around. But they don't know. You can't seem to talk about what happened in your life.

Some of you have gone through divorces, tragedies, and adulterous relationships, and you've been left feeling unwanted. You can't shout over that sort of thing. You can't leap over that kind of wall. It injures something about you that changes how you relate to everyone else for the rest of your life.

What do you do when you are trapped in a transitory state, neither in nor out? You're left lying at the door, torn up and disturbed, trembling and intimidated. What do you do when you don't know what to do?

There's a call out in the Spirit for hurting women. The Lord says, "I want you." No matter how many men have told you, "I don't want you," God says, "I want you. I've seen you bent over. I've seen the aftereffects of what happened to you. I've seen you at your worst moment. I still want you." God has not changed His mind. God loves with an everlasting love.

YOUR HEALING JOURNEY

Perhaps the greatest lie you can believe is "God doesn't want you anymore." To believe this deception is even worse than the sin that invited the condemning thoughts. Why? Sin is common to all. In the church, out of the church— Jesus died on the Cross, not just to forgive the sins of your past, but to offer forgiveness for the present and future. Just because you invited Jesus into your life, go to church, and try to live the Christian life does not mean you are excluded from sin. Not by a long shot. Jesus paid the price knowing completely what He was getting into with you. He knew you'd fall, stumble, and make the mistakes you did. The question is not, "Will I fall?" Rather, the question is, "How will I respond when I fall?"

In the wake of pain and abuse, hurt and shame, sin and guilt, it becomes easy to believe the condemning voice of the accuser. This is why Scriptures like Romans 8:1 should be spiritual lifelines for you. If the enemy can make you believe that God is through with you, you will begin living like God is through with you. That's a demonic, destructive lie, but it will become your reality if you cling to it as fact.

Here is what you need to do. Right now, honestly bring your guilt and shame to God. Every act, every thought, every past incident, and every present struggle you have— bring it openly before the Lord of Heaven and Earth. He sees all, so it is useless trying to hide anything from Him. Simply pray like this,

> *God, the Bible says there is no condemnation for those in Christ Jesus.*
>
> *I reject the lie that I am not in Christ because of what I've done (am doing).*
>
> *Right now, I recognize that as a lie of the enemy, not a prompting of the Spirit.*
>
> *I repent for my sins.*
>
> *I lay my past before You.*

I present my shame, my guilt, and my striving to cover it all up.

Right now, I ask you to cover me in the precious blood of Jesus, for His blood made atonement for every single sin.

You see and know everything; nothing is hidden from Your sight. And still You love me. Still you call me back home. Still you invite me into Your holy presence. I receive this, not because of how good I am, but because of how good You are!

I may not feel clean, worthy, or forgiven, but Your Word says that I am.

I may feel condemned, but I stand righteous in Your sight because of Jesus's blood.

I may feel unwanted…but You still want me!

Thank You, Lord, that there is no condemnation for those who are in Christ…and I am in Christ!

THE LORD SEES AND WANTS YOU

And when Jesus saw her, he called her to him....
—LUKE 13:12

When Jesus encountered the infirm woman of Luke 13, He called out to her. There may have been many fine women present that day, but the Lord didn't call them forward. He reached around all of them and found that crippled woman in the back. He called forth the wounded, hurting woman with a past. He issued the Spirit's call to those who had their value and self-esteem destroyed by the intrusion of vicious circumstances.

The infirm woman must have thought, *He wants me. He wants me. I'm frayed and torn, but He wants me. I have been through trouble. I have been through this trauma, but He wants me.* Perhaps she thought no one would ever want her again, but Jesus wanted her. He had a plan.

She may have known that it would take a while for her life to be completely put back together. She had many things to overcome. She was handicapped. She was probably filled with insecurities. Yet Jesus still called her forth for His touch.

If you can identify with the feelings of this infirm woman, then know that He's waiting on you and that He wants you. He sees your struggling and He knows all about your pain. He knows what happened to you 18 years ago or 10 years ago or even last week. With patience He waits for you, as the father waited for the prodigal son. Jesus says to the hurting and crippled, "I want you enough to wait for you to hobble your way back home."

Now God says, "I'm going to deliver you and heal you. Now I'm going to renew you and release you. I'm going to tell you who you really are. Now I'm ready to reveal to you why you had to go through what you did to become what you shall become." He says, "Now I'm going to tell you a secret, something between you and Me no one else knows. Your boyfriend didn't know, your first husband didn't know. I'll tell you something that your father, uncle, brother, or whoever abused you had no knowledge of. Just realize that you are the daughter of a king. Your Father is the King."

YOUR HEALING JOURNEY

You are moving in a divine flow of grace right now. I pray you sense it. Yesterday, you dealt with the major barrier to your advancement and complete healing—condemnation. Condemnation produces rejection, and rejection keeps us in bondage to the destructive cycles that have been oppressing us. When we believe we are rejected by God, we go back to familiar places (and people) that "accepted us." This is why the lie that "God has rejected you" is so dangerous. When we believe God doesn't want us or see us anymore, we will go back to anyone or anything that even gives us some sense of acceptance. It's natural for people to want to be accepted. The problem is when we do not have that foundational source of acceptance (the love of God) flowing into our lives on a consistent basis. This is, once again, why condemnation is so costly.

Remember, you are in Christ! Believe this. It doesn't come by your good deeds or religious attempts at cleaning up. You are in Christ because the blood of Jesus made a very expensive payment for you. You are in Christ because God put you there! Is it possible to stop being in Christ? There are many different theologies about this—none of which we need to explore today, as they are irrelevant to the topic.

The greatest danger comes when we stop believing that we are in Christ. This is what begins the downward spiral, either into greater sin, addiction, bondage, fear, etc. Just like the Lord saw and called forth the infirm woman, He is doing the same today. Whatever put you in the "infirm" category, it doesn't matter. Lift up your head...the Healer is calling you!

Day Thirty-One

LIVE IN THE "NOW" OF FREEDOM

So if the Son sets you free, you are
free through and through.
—JOHN 8:36, MSG

When the infirm woman came to Jesus, He proclaimed her freedom. Now she stands erect for the first time in 18 years. When you come to Jesus, He will cause you to stand in His strength. You will know how important you are to Him. Part of your recovery is to learn how to stand up and live in the "now" of life instead of the "then" of yesterday. That was then, but this is now.

I proclaim to the abused: There is a healing going into your spirit right now.

I speak life to you.

I speak deliverance to you.

I speak restoration to you. All in the mighty name of Jesus, in the invincible, all-powerful, everlasting name of Jesus.

I proclaim victory to you.

You will recover the loss you suffered at the hands of your abuser.

You will get back every stolen item.

He will heal that broken twig.

He will rebuild your self-esteem, your self-respect, and your integrity.

All you need do is allow His power and anointing to touch the hurting places. He will take care of the secrets. He touches the places where you've been assassinated. He knows the woman you would have been, the woman you should have been, the woman you could have been. God is healing and restoring her in you as you call out to Him.

The enemy wanted to change your destiny through a series of events, but God will restore you to wholeness as if the events had never happened. The triumphant woman locked inside shall come forth to where she belongs. He's delivering her. He's releasing her. He's restoring her. He's building her back. He's bringing her out. He's delivering by the power of His Spirit.

YOUR HEALING JOURNEY

Freedom is available to you right now! Reach out and receive it. Everything that you just read—the prayers and declarations of freedom—are yours. We've established you are worthy to receive them, not because of your works but because of Jesus. You're worthy to be free. You're worthy to walk in the perfect freedom provided by the Son of God.

Sometimes, the enemy tries to convince us we are not worthy of the freedom that Jesus made available. We've gone too far. We've done too much. We've missed too many opportunities. We've stumbled too often. We've left the God we loved. We're not like we used to be. Any of these lies starting to sound familiar? Every lie is aimed at you with the intention of deceiving you right out of your freedom.

The devil is a liar and he knows that the only way he can try to short-circuit your freedom is bombarding you with his lies. He's desperate for you to believe a lie because it's costly to him if you start believing the truth. Right now, I declare in Jesus's name that you pick up the Sword of the Spirit, the Word of God, and you begin to swing it with full force and authority at every fiery dart of the enemy. Scripture tells us that this weapon of the Word extinguishes his attempts to destroy you, primarily through deception.

The Word is Truth. Final. Definitive. Unchanging. The enemy comes with lies that are subject to the measuring rod of Scripture. Every lie that he sends your way that disagrees with the Word of God is fit to be cut down. Destroyed. Extinguished. Receive the Truth of God's Word right now, as this is the key to unlocking your freedom in Christ!

Day Thirty-Two

CALL OUT TO JESUS

*Not by might, nor by power, but by
my spirit, saith the Lord of hosts.*
—ZECHARIAH 4:6

The anointing of the living God is reaching out to you. He calls you forth to set you free. When you reach out to Him and allow the Holy Spirit to have His way, His anointing is present to deliver you. Demons will tremble. Satan wants to keep you at the door but never let you enter. He wants to keep you down. Now his power is broken in your life.

Jesus said, "*The Spirit of the Lord is upon me, because he hath anointed me to preach the gospel to the poor; he hath sent me to heal the brokenhearted, to preach deliverance to the captives, and recovering of sight to the blind, to set at liberty them that are bruised*" (Luke 4:18).

You may have thought that you would never rejoice again. God declares that you can have freedom in Him—now! The joy that He brings can be restored to your soul. He identifies with your pain and suffering. He knows what it is like to suffer abuse at the hands of others. Yet He proclaims joy and strength. He will give you the garment of praise instead of the spirit of heaviness (see Isa. 61:3).

Once you have called out to Him, you can lift up your hands in praise. No matter what you have suffered, you can hold up your head. Regardless of who has hurt you, hold up your head! Forget how many times you've been married. Put aside those who mistreated you. You may have been a lesbian. You may have been a crack addict. It doesn't matter who you were. You may have even been molested. You can't change where you have been, but you can change where you are going.

YOUR HEALING JOURNEY

The only way you are going to experience true, sustained freedom in your life is through the power of the Holy Spirit. You need His divine ability, as you are unable to do it yourself. You may have tried, but I'm sure you've failed. We all fail at trying to do God's job for Him, as He is the only One qualified to set us free…and keep us free.

So, what do you do now?

Call out to Jesus.

Lift up your voice without shame, fear, or intimidation.

Draw near to God and He will draw near to you!

Simply ask the Spirit of God to empower you to move beyond your past, let go of condemnation, receive His forgiveness, and embrace the healing He wants to bring to every area of your life that is hurting.

Just remember, you are qualified to call upon the name of the Lord and receive His power. That is the only way that you will experience the freedom you long for!

Day Thirty-Three

STEP INTO YOUR RESTORATION!

Lift up your heads, O ye gates; even lift them
up, ye everlasting doors; and the King of glory
shall come in. Who is this King of glory? The
Lord of hosts, he is the King of glory. Selah.
—PSALM 24:9-10

The Lord will restore to you that which the cankerworm and the locust ate up (see Joel 2:25). He said, "I'm going to give it back to you." Maybe you wrestle with guilt. You've had abortions. You've been hearing babies crying in your spirit. You feel so dirty. You've been misused and abused. The devil keeps bringing up to you your failures of the past.

> *Come now, and let us reason together, saith the*
> *Lord: though your sins be as scarlet, they shall be as*
> *white as snow; though they be red like crimson, they*
> *shall be as wool* (Isaiah 1:18).

All my life I have had a tremendous compassion for hurting people. When other people would put their foot on them,

I always tended to have a ministry of mercy. Perhaps it is because I've had my own pain. When you have suffered, it makes you able to relate to other people's pain. The Lord settled me in a ministry that just tends to cater to hurting people. Sometimes when I minister, I find myself fighting back tears. Sometimes I can hear the cries of anguished people in the crowd.

You're a survivor.

You should celebrate your survival. Instead of agonizing over your tragedies, you should celebrate your victory and thank God you made it. I charge you to step over your adversity and walk into the newness. It is like stepping from a storm into the sunshine. Just step into it now.

YOUR HEALING JOURNEY

You've survived your past. You've made it through your pain. Now, it's time for you to advance! God wants to release restoration into your life for everything you've suffered, everything you lost. Remember, Heaven's restoration always comes with interest. He restores double what was stolen from you!

Claim these promises as your own:

Come back to the place of safety, all you prisoners who still have hope! I promise this very day that I will repay two blessings for each of your troubles (Zechariah 9:12 NLT).

Instead of your shame you will receive a double portion, and instead of disgrace you will rejoice in your inheritance (Isaiah 61:7 NIV).

Receive these promises as your own today!

WALK IN THE NEWNESS OF LIFE

And just as Christ was raised from the
dead by the glorious power of the Father,
now we also may live new lives.
—ROMANS 6:4, NLT

God has blessed me with two little boys and two little daughters. As a father, I have found that I have a ministry of hugs. When something happens and I really can't fix it, I just hug them. I can't change how other people treated them. I can't change what happened at school. I can't make the teacher like them. I can't take away the insults. But I can hug them!

I believe the best nurses are the ones who have been patients. They have compassion on the victim. If anyone understands the plight of women, it ought to be women. The Church needs to develop a ministry of hugs. The touch of the Master sets us free. The touch of a fellow pilgrim lets us know we are not alone in our plight.

The Holy Spirit is calling for the broken, infirm women to come to Jesus. He will restore and deliver. How do we come to Jesus? We come to His Body, the Church. It is in the Church that we can hear the Word of God. The Church gives us strength and nourishment. The Church is to be the place where we share our burdens and allow others to help us with them. The Spirit calls; the burdened need only heed the call.

There are three tenses of faith! When Lazarus died, Martha, his sister, said, "Lord, if You would have been here, my brother would not have died." This is historical faith. Its view is digressive.

Then when Jesus said, "Lazarus will live again," his sister replied, "I know he will live in the resurrection." This is futuristic faith. It is progressive.

Martha says, "But *even now* You have the power to raise him up again." (See John 11:21-27.) I feel like Martha.

Even now, after all you've been through, God has the power to raise you up again! This is the present tense of faith. Walk into your newness even now.

YOUR HEALING JOURNEY

For too many people, Christian salvation is a theology, not a reality. They understand the biblical and scriptural language of being "forgiven of sin" and living a new life. Even in the practice of baptism, we allow profound and life-altering truths to be reduced to ritual. We were buried in the death of Christ and raised to walk in the newness of life through His resurrection. We know the "church" language all too well, but sadly we do not walk in the experience well enough.

Start living your salvation today! Jesus set you free. Decide in your mind that you will start thinking like a free person. You will start speaking like a free person. You will start looking at yourself like a free person. No longer will your past or bondage define you. That is not who you are. I don't care if your "past" happened twenty years ago or it happened last night, that is not who you are. You are a new creation in Jesus Christ. You are a redeemed and blood-bought daughter of God.

It's not enough to sign off on a church's statement of core values, professing that you believe these truths; it's time for you to begin experiencing their power in your everyday life!

YOU ARE WORTHY OF COVENANT

Live a life worthy of the Lord and please him in every way: bearing fruit in every good work, growing in the knowledge of God.
—COLOSSIANS 1:10, NIV

Nearly every home in America is wired for electricity. Walls are covered with receptacles which deliver the electric current. In order to take advantage of the power, something must be plugged into the receptacle. The receptacle is the female and the plug is the male.

Women were made like receptacles. They were made to be receivers. Men were made to be givers, physically, sexually, and emotionally, by providing for others. In every area, women were made to receive.

The woman was made, fashioned out of the man, to be a help meet. Through their union, they find wholeness in each other. She helps him meet and accomplish his task. In other words, if you have a power saw, it has great potential for cutting. However, it is ineffective until it is plugged in. The receptacle helps the power saw meet its purpose. Without that receptacle, the power saw, although mighty, remains limited.

However, there is a vulnerability about the receptacle. The vulnerability exists because receptacles must be careful what kind of plug they are connected with. Receptacles are open. Women are open by nature and design. Men are closed. You must be careful what you allow to plug into you and draw strength from you. The wrong plugs may seek your help and drain your power.

God recognizes your vulnerability; therefore, He has designed that the one who plugs into a woman sexually will have a covenant with that woman. God never intended for humanity to have casual sex. His design always included the commitment of a covenant. He purposed that a man who has sexual relations with a woman would be committed to that same woman for life. Nothing short of this commitment meets His standard. God wants you covered, like an outlet is covered, in order that no one tamper with your intended purpose. The married woman is covered by her husband. The single woman is covered by her chastity and morality. It is dangerous to be uncovered.

YOUR HEALING JOURNEY

To sustain freedom in your life—especially when it comes to matters of relationships and sexuality—it is vital that you recognize that you are worthy of covenant. This will help you successfully evaluate what kind of people you allow into your life when it comes to developing relationships.

The man who truly recognizes that you are worthy of a covenant is a man worth getting into relationship with. Even if the relationship does not progress to marriage and you both discover that it doesn't work, at least he will ensure you that are appropriately protected.

Your purity is a gift. If you've fallen and compromised in the past, there is no condemnation. There is no second-class citizenship in the Kingdom of God. This is such a delicate topic of discussion because of how much fear-mongering has been associated with the message of purity, sexual abstinence, and saving yourself until marriage.

It has little to do with dos and don'ts and everything to do with how you see yourself. If you believe you are valuable, you will pursue purity. Whether you've had numerous sexual relationships in the past or have never even kissed a man, see yourself as pure. As clean before the Lord. This is your identity, and when you discover that this is who you are in Christ, you will never for settle for any man in any relationship who tries to lure you into compromise.

Daughter of God, you are worthy of the commitment of covenant!

WHO IS UNCOVERING YOU?

And God said, Let us make man in our image,
after our likeness: and let them have dominion over
the fish of the sea, and over the fowl of the air, and
over the cattle, and over all the earth, and over
every creeping thing that creepeth upon the earth.
—GENESIS 1:26

Originally, God created humanity perfect and good. God placed Adam in the garden He had prepared for him. The only rule was man should not eat of the tree of the knowledge of good and evil. God wanted mankind to rely on Him for moral decisions. After the Fall, history records the consequences of man trying to make moral decisions for himself.

Although God had made a wonderful place for Adam to live, the man remained less than complete. He needed a woman. Keep in mind, though, that she completed his purpose, not his person. If you're not complete as a person, marriage will not help you.

And the Lord God caused a deep sleep to fall upon Adam, and he slept: and he took one of his ribs, and closed up the flesh instead thereof; and the rib, which the Lord God had taken from man, made he a woman, and brought her unto the man (Genesis 2:21-22).

In Genesis chapter 3, we see that Eve allowed herself to be taken advantage of by satan, who plugged into her desire to see, taste, and be wise. The enemy took advantage of her weakness. *"And the man said, The woman whom thou gavest to be with me, she gave me of the tree, and I did eat"* (Gen. 3:12).

Eve had given her attention over to someone else. *"And the Lord God said unto the woman, What is this that thou hast done? And the woman said, The serpent beguiled me, and I did eat"* (Gen. 3:13). Adam's anger is shown by his statement, "You gave her to be with me." The woman answered, "Well, I couldn't help it. He plugged into me, or he beguiled me."

You've got to be careful who you let uncover you, because they can lead you to complete destruction.

YOUR HEALING JOURNEY

This journey is one of spiritual warfare. Even though this topic is not popular in many circles today, it is vital for you to be on the lookout for the serpent's craftiness. He is at war against the daughters of God. He is out to lure you into temptation with the purpose of uncovering you. He wants you shamed. He wants you falling down so he can immediately swoop in with condemnation.

Already, we have dealt with the thoughts of condemnation the enemy tries to bring against you. He is an accuser. That is his very nature. Once you get over one bout of condemnation, the devil is looking for another opportunity to bring you in. He wants you to live under the heavy yoke of condemnation so that you are rendered incapacitated. He does not want you functioning as the woman God ordained you to be, because your purpose fulfilled means his destruction. As you walk in your destiny, by default, ground is being advanced for the Kingdom of God and displaced from the enemy.

PLUG INTO PRAYER AND SHIFT THE ATMOSPHERE

And the Lord God said unto the serpent, Because thou hast done this, thou art cursed above all cattle, and above every beast of the field; upon thy belly shalt thou go, and dust shalt thou eat all the days of thy life: and I will put enmity between thee and the woman, and between thy seed and her seed; and it shall bruise thy head, and thou shalt bruise his heel.
—GENESIS 3:14-15

There is a special enmity between femininity and the enemy. There is a special conflict between the woman and the enemy. That's why you must do spiritual warfare. You must do spiritual warfare against the enemy because you are vulnerable in certain areas and there is enmity between you and the enemy.

You must be on your guard. Women tend to be more prayerful than men, once they are committed. If you are a woman living today and you're not learning spiritual warfare, you're in trouble. The enemy may be taking advantage of you.

He is attracted to you because he knows that you were designed as a receptacle to help meet someone's vision. If he can get you to help meet his vision, you will have great problems. God said, *"And I will put enmity between thee and the woman, and between thy seed and her seed"* (Gen. 3:15).

Now, God didn't say only "her seed and your seed." He said, "Between you and the woman." There is a fight between you and the devil. Who are the victims of the most rapes in this country? Who are the victims of the most child abuse? Who are the victims of much of the sexual discrimination in the job market? Who has the most trouble getting together, unifying with each other, and collaborating? Over and over again, satan is attacking and assaulting your femininity.

Satan is continually attacking women. If godly women do not learn how to start praying and doing effective spiritual warfare, they will not discern what is plugging into them. Perhaps you become completely vulnerable to moods and attitudes and dispositions. Perhaps you are doing things and you don't know why. Something's plugging into you. If you are tempted to rationalize, "I'm just in a bad mood. I don't know just what it is. I'm just evil. I'm tough," don't believe it. Something's plugging into you.

YOUR HEALING JOURNEY

To be victorious over the enemy, you must first be aware that he is against you. He's against you because he fears your capacity as an atmosphere-shifter. He is continually, relentlessly attacking women. You just reviewed some of the different horrible ways he does this. Why is the devil's assault against women so vicious? He knows the power of what happens when you become plugged into your purpose. He also knows what happens when you respond to the static in the atmosphere with prayer and intercession. Women know something about prayer because they are familiar with the process of birthing.

Everything that Heaven releases into the earth comes through the womb of prayer. Prayer ushers people into the Kingdom of God. Prayer releases healing. Prayer breaks bondages. Prayer changes outcomes. Prayer shifts atmospheres. Why is prayer so vital? Because it's the vehicle through which people partner with God.

When you start to pick up on things in the environment, don't just assume you're going crazy. Don't think, "I'm just in a bad mood," or "I'm feeling off today." Women are highly perceptive to spiritual atmospheres. The enemy tries to get you to identify with the spiritual climate of the atmosphere. Don't do this. Instead, shift the atmosphere through prayer. If you sense spiritual static around you, don't receive it; pray against it.

Release the peace of God, the blessing of God, the Kingdom of God through prayer. Pray under your breath if you need to. Pray silently. Pray in your mind. Doesn't matter how you pray—just pray and believe that your prayers are changing the atmosphere around you.

IDENTIFY THE BIRTH CANAL

Unto the woman he said, I will greatly multiply
thy sorrow and thy conception; in sorrow thou
shalt bring forth children; and thy desire shall
be to thy husband, and he shall rule over thee.
—GENESIS 3:16

God wasn't finished with His pronouncements to the serpent after the Fall. Next He addressed Eve directly.

The Lord explained that birthing comes through sorrow. Everything you bring forth comes through pain. If it didn't come through pain, it probably wasn't worth much. If you're going to bring forth—and I'm not merely talking about babies, I'm talking about birthing vision and purpose—you will do so with sorrow and pain. If you're going to bring forth anything in your career, your marriage, or your life; if you're going to develop anything in your character; if you're going to be a fruitful woman it's going to come through sorrow. It will come through the things you suffer. You will enter into strength through sorrow.

Sorrow is not the object; it's simply the canal that the object comes through. Many of you are mistaking sorrow for the baby instead of the canal. In that case, all you have is pain. You ought to have a child for every sorrow. For every sorrow, for every intense groaning in your spirit, you ought to have something to show for it. Don't let the devil give you sorrow without seed. Any time you have sorrow, it is a sign that God is trying to get something through you and to you.

Be careful that you don't walk away with the pain and leave the baby in the store. You are the producers. You are the ones through whom life passes. Every child who enters into this world must come through you. Even Jesus Christ had to come through a woman to get legal entry into the world. He had to come through you.

You are a channel and an expression of blessings. If there is to be any virtue, any praise, any victory, any deliverance, it's got to come through you.

Satan wants to use you as a legal entry into this world or into your family. That's how he destroyed the human race with the first family. He knows that you are the entrance of all things. You are the doors of life. Be careful what you let come through you. Close the doors to the planting of the enemy. Then know that when travail comes into your spirit, it's because you're going to give birth.

YOUR HEALING JOURNEY

Pain and sorrow come with the territory of being a life-bearer. Any mother in the natural will tell you that the process of childbirth comes with a certain amount of physical sorrow to the body. The pain is not the end goal of the birthing process, though. The life is. There is life on the other side of the sorrow you have been experiencing. It's easy to want to give up in response to the pain. Some people even mistakenly believe that the pain is God's end result of the process.

God is not a sadist; anything painful that we experience along our life journey is purposed to birth new things and usher us into greater levels of glory. Don't mistake the pain of the birth canal for the beautiful life that will be brought forth as a result.

I remind you, life is on the other side of your pain and sorrow. Don't give up. Don't let the pain cause you to stop moving forward on you journey. Know that God will work all things together for your good. Anytime the enemy wants you to respond to pain by giving up, just remember that the presence of pain means new life is passing through the birth canal!

HOLD THE PRIZE, DROP THE PAIN

*But one thing I do: Forgetting what is behind
and straining toward what is ahead.*
—PHILIPPIANS 3:13, NIV

You will give birth! That's why you have suffered pain. Your spirit is signaling you that something is trying to get through. Don't become so preoccupied with the pain that you forget to push the baby. Sometimes you're pushing the pain and not the baby, and you're so engrossed with what's hurting you that you're not doing what it takes to produce fruit in your life.

When you see sorrow multiply, it is a sign that God is getting ready to send something to you. Don't settle for the pain and not get the benefit. Hold out. Disregard the pain and get the promise. Understand that God has promised some things to you that He wants you to have, and you've got to stay there on the table until you get to the place where you ought to be in the Lord. After all, the pain is forgotten when the baby is born.

What is the pain when compared with the baby? Some may have dropped the baby. That happens when you become so engrossed with the pain that you leave the reward behind you. Your attention gets focused on the wrong thing. You can be so preoccupied with how bad it hurts that you miss the joy of a vision giving birth.

Wouldn't it be a foolish thing for a woman to go into labor, go through all of the pain, stay on the delivery table, stay in labor for hours and hours, and simply get up and walk out of the hospital? It would be foolish for her to concentrate on the pain to the extent that she would leave the baby lying in the hospital. However, that is exactly what happens when you become preoccupied with how bad the past hurts you. Maybe you have walked away and left the baby lying on the floor.

For every struggle in your life, God accomplished something in your character and in your spirit. Why hold the pain and drop the baby when you could hold the baby and drop the pain? You are holding on to the wrong thing if all you do is concentrate on past pain. Release the pain. Pain doesn't fall off on its own. It's got to be released. Release the pain. Allow God to loose you from the pain and separate you from what has afflicted you, and be left with the baby and not the problem.

YOUR HEALING JOURNEY

How do you effectively let go of what's behind you? You cannot totally forget the past, so you need to reorient your focus. For too many, the past is strictly associated with pain. It's time to move past the pain of yesterday and adjust your attention to see what was birthed. Remember, sorrow is a birthing canal. Suffering represented transition. You need to change your perspective in order to be developed by something that tried to destroy you.

This is the ultimate way we deprive the enemy of any victory in our lives. Even the tactics he used hoping to take us out become part of our journey to breakthrough, growth, and maturity.

PUSH!

I push hard toward what is ahead of me.
—PHILIPPIANS 3:13, NIRV

God said to the woman, "*In sorrow thou shalt bring forth children*" (Gen. 3:16). That includes every area of your life. That's true in your character. That's true in your personality. It is true in your spirit as well as in your finances. Bring forth, ladies! If it comes into this world, it has to come through you. If you're in a financial rut, bring forth. If you're in need of healing for your body, bring forth. Understand that it must be brought forth. It doesn't just happen by accident.

The midwife tells a woman, "Push." The baby will not come forth if you don't push him. God will not allow you to become trapped in a situation without escape. But you've got to push while you are in pain if you intend to produce. I'm told that when the pain is at its height, that's when they instruct you to push, not when the pain recedes. When the pain is at its ultimate expression, that is the time you need to push.

As you begin to push in spite of the pain, the pain recedes into the background because you become preoccupied with the change rather than the problem. Push! You don't have time to cry. Push! You don't have time to be suicidal. Push! This is not the time to give up. Push, because God is about to birth a promise through you. Cry if you must, and groan if you have to, but keep on pushing because God has promised that if it is to come into the world, it's got to pass through you.

There remains a conflict between past pain and future desire. Here is the conflict. He said, "*in sorrow thou shalt bring forth children; and thy desire shall be to thy husband, and he shall rule over thee*" (Gen. 3:16). In other words, you have so much pain in producing the child that, if you don't have balance between past pain and future desire, you will quit producing. God says, "After the pain, your desire shall be to your husband." Pain is swallowed by desire.

Impregnated with destiny, women of promise must bear down in the spirit. The past hurts; the pain is genuine. However, you must learn to get in touch with something other than your pain. If you do not have desire, you won't have the tenacity to resurrect. Desire will come back. After the pain is over, desire follows, because it takes desire to be productive again.

YOUR HEALING JOURNEY

The key to producing is pushing. To move beyond your past, you need to push. To move toward your destiny, you need to push. To outlast disappointment and discouragement, you need to push.

Pushing is your key to outlasting adversity.

Push your way into the future.

Push past the pain.

Push right into promise!

Why do you need to push? Because you have an enemy who brings adversity. It's a part of life. No one is excluded from dealing with adversity and resistance and suffering. That is common. What's uncommon is the woman who decides to push through!

A VISION TO MOVE FORWARD

And the Lord answered me: "Write the vision; make it plain on tablets, so he may run who reads it."
—HABAKKUK 2:2, ESV

I have been in the delivery room with my wife as she was giving birth. I witnessed the pain and suffering she endured. I believe that there were times of such intense pain that she would have shot me if she had had a chance. Her desire made her continue. She didn't simply give up. She endured the pain so new life could be born. Once the child was born, the pain was soon forgotten.

Until the desire to go forward becomes greater than the memories of past pain, you will never hold the power to create again. However, when the desire comes back into your spirit and begins to live in you again, it will release you from the pain.

God wants to give us the strength to overcome past pain and move forward into new life. Solomon wrote, *"Where there is no vision, the people perish"* (Prov. 29:18). Vision is the desire to go ahead. Until you have a vision to go ahead, you will always live in yesterday's struggles. God is calling you to today. The devil wants you to live in yesterday. He's always telling you about what you cannot do. His method is to bring up your past. He wants to draw your attention backward.

God wants to put desire in the spirit of broken women. There wouldn't be any desire if there wasn't any relationship. You can't desire something that's not there. The very fact that you have a desire is in itself an indication that better days are coming. David said, "*I had fainted, unless I had believed to see the goodness of the Lord in the land of the living*" (Ps. 27:13).

Expect something wonderful to happen!

YOUR HEALING JOURNEY

Vision is everything when it comes to moving forward in your life. One of the most surefire ways that you can move beyond the constraints and bondages of the past is get a clear vision for your future. Right now, I encourage you to ask the Lord:

Father, I pray You would give me a clear vision for the future that You envision for me.

It's a future without fear and a future without bondage.

It's a future without guilt and shame.

It's a future where my past no longer haunts me, but helps me.

127

My past is no longer a topic that brings me anxiety.
When I share my story, Your grace is on it.
It's not a story of hurt, but of healing.
Thank You, God, that you take ashes and make them into something beautiful.
I ask You to do this even in this very moment.
In Jesus's Name, Amen!

Don't end with this prayer! In fact, this prayer represents another new beginning as you go on this healing journey. Continue to ask God to show you His version of your future. It's important that you consult the Healer, not your history, on what your future looks like.

A VISION OF POSSIBILITY AND POWER

I can do all things through Christ
who strengthens me.
—PHILIPPIANS 4:13, NKJV

When I was a boy, we had a dog named Pup. Don't let the name fool you, though. He was a mean and ferocious animal. He would eat anyone who came near him. We had him chained in the back of the house to a four-by-four post. The chain was huge. We never imagined that he could possibly tear himself loose from that post. He would chase something and the chain would snap him back. We often laughed at him as we stood outside his reach.

One day Pup saw something that he really wanted. It was out of his reach. However, the motivation before him became more important than what was behind him. He pulled that chain to the limit. All at once, instead of drawing him back, the chain snapped, and Pup was loose to chase his prey.

That's what God will do for you. The thing that used to pull you back will snap, and you will be liberated by a goal because God has put greatness before you. You can't receive what God wants for your life by looking back. He is mighty. He is powerful enough to destroy the yoke of the enemy in your life. He is strong enough to bring you out and loose you, deliver you, and set you free.

What we need is a seed in the womb that we believe is enough to produce an embryo. We must be willing to feed that embryo for it to grow and become visible. When it will not be hidden anymore, it will break forth in life as answered prayer. It will break forth. No matter how hard others try to hold it back, it will break forth.

Put the truth in your spirit and feed, nurture, and allow it to grow. Quit telling yourself, "You're too fat, too old, too late, or too ignorant." Quit feeding yourself that garbage. That will not nourish the baby. Too often we starve the embryo of faith that is growing within us. It is unwise to speak against your own body. Women tend to speak against their bodies, opening the door for sickness and disease. Speak life to your own body. Celebrate who you are.

You are the image of God!

YOUR HEALING JOURNEY

You are made in the image of God! Even more so, this incredible, extraordinary, and supernatural God lives inside of you! There is nothing off-limits to the power of God, correct? If there is nothing off-limits to Him, then there is nothing off-limits to you because you are made in His image and filled with His very Spirit! Let truth like this define your vision moving forward.

YOUR LIFE-GIVING SOURCE OF POWER AND STRENGTH

Man shall not live by bread alone, but by every word that proceedeth out of the mouth of God.
—MATTHEW 4:4

Scriptures remind us of who we are. *"I will praise Thee; for I am fearfully and wonderfully made: marvellous are thy works; and that my soul knoweth right well"* (Ps. 139:14). These are the words that will feed our souls. The truth will allow new life to swell up within us. Feed the embryo within with such words as these.

When I consider thy heavens, the work of thy fingers, the moon and the stars, which thou hast ordained; what is man, that thou art mindful of him? and the son of man, that thou visitest him? (Psalm 8:3-4)

And the Lord shall make thee the head, and not the tail; and thou shalt be above only, and thou shalt not be beneath (Deuteronomy 28:13).

I can do all things through Christ which strengtheneth me (Philippians 4:13).

The Word of God will provide the nourishment that will feed the baby inside.

The Book of Hebrews provides us with a tremendous lesson on faith. When we believe God, we are counted as righteous. Righteousness cannot be earned or merited. It comes only through faith. We can have a good report simply on the basis of our faith. Faith becomes the tender, like money is the legal tender in this world that we use for exchange of goods and services. Faith becomes the tender, or the substance, of things hoped for, and the evidence of things not seen. By it the elders obtained a good report (see Heb. 11:1-2).

"Through faith we understand that the worlds were framed by the word of God, so that things which are seen were not made of things which do appear" (Heb. 11:3). The invisible became visible and was manifested. God wants us to understand that just because we can't see it, doesn't mean that He won't do it. What God wants to do in us begins as a word that gets in the spirit. Everything that is tangible started as an intangible. It was a dream, a thought, a word of God. In the same way, what man has invented began as a concept in someone's mind. So just because we don't see it, doesn't mean we won't get it.

YOUR HEALING JOURNEY

During this part of your healing journey, I want you to focus on building vision. One of the ways you develop new vision for your future is by nourishing yourself on the Word of God. This is your life-giving source of power and strength. The Word of God gives you the ability to take trauma and turn it into testimony. How is this even possible? It's no magic trick or formula. Scripture introduces you to the thoughts of a Redeeming God. Redemption does not overlook what happened to you, in the same way that God does not simply pretend you were never hurt. When you hurt, He hurts. He is ever near to the broken. While living mindful of His closeness in difficult times, you must also lift your eyes and begin to see God's redemptive vision for your past. For your trial. For your pain. For your hurt. For the horrors that were committed against you or perhaps the sins that you willingly participated in. It doesn't matter who was responsible or whose fault it was. God's redemptive vision seeks to take the pain of your past and give it Heaven's purpose.

Does this mean God intentionally caused or divinely orchestrated your pain? Certainly not. God is not the author of such things; however, He is the Redeemer. Every area of your life that was broken, He wants to enter and release Heaven's wholeness. I encourage you to have vision for a God who sees no area of your life as off-limits. There is no one and nothing beyond the reach of His redemptive power!

BY FAITH...

*Now faith is the substance of things hoped
for, the evidence of things not seen. For by
it the elders obtained a good report.*
—HEBREWS 11:1-2

There is a progression in the characters mentioned in this chapter of Hebrews. Abel worshiped God by faith. Enoch walked with God by faith. You can't walk with God until you worship God. The first calling is to learn how to worship God. When you learn how to worship God, then you can develop a walk with God. Stop trying to get people to walk with God who won't worship. If you don't love Him enough to worship, you'll never be able to walk with Him. If you can worship like Abel, then you can walk like Enoch.

Enoch walked, and by faith Noah worked with God. You can't work with God until you walk with God. You can't walk with God until you worship God. If you can worship like Abel, then you can walk like Enoch. And if you walk like Enoch, then you can work like Noah.

But without faith it is impossible to please him: for he that cometh to God must believe that he is, and that he is a rewarder of them that diligently seek him (Hebrews 11:6).

God will reward those who persevere in seeking Him. He may not come when you want Him to, but He will be right on time. If you will wait on the Lord, He will strengthen your heart. He will heal you and deliver you. He will lift you up and break those chains. God's power will loose the bands from around your neck. He will give you the garment of praise for the spirit of heaviness (see Isa. 61:3).

YOUR HEALING JOURNEY

It all begins with worship. Worship God. Don't limit this concept of worship to what goes on during a Sunday morning church service. Worship does not begin with a song, a choir, or a music team; it begins with a heart that beholds God Almighty. To gaze upon the glory, power, might, and love of God, you are truly left with no alternative but to worship.

Surely, this begs the question, "Why don't more people truly worship God?" Many haven't taken the time to behold Him. It's not about participating in religious ritual or spiritual activity for the sake of trying to accomplish something for God. So many people are imprisoned to the idea of working for God without worshiping God. And plus, you are not really working for God—like Noah, you work with God. God doesn't need anyone to work for Him; He seeks friends and intimates who work with Him.

Worship represents a heart that says an abandoned "Yes" to everything that God is and everything God says. Worship ignites a lifestyle of faith. When you know who God truly is, your only fitting response to what He asks of you is "Yes." Even when it doesn't make sense and absolutely boggles your mind, we respond in faith…to the God we know, the God we love, the God we trust, and the God we worship.

Day Forty-Five

BE A WOMB-MAN

By faith Abraham, when he was called to go out into a place which he should after receive for an inheritance, obeyed; and he went out, not knowing whither he went.
—HEBREWS 11:8

Abraham was a great man of faith. The writer of Hebrews mentions many areas of Abraham's faith. Abraham looked for a city whose builder and maker was God (see Heb. 11:10). However, he is not listed in the faith "hall of fame" as the one who produced Isaac. If Abraham was famous for anything, it should have been for producing Isaac. However, he is not applauded for that.

"*Through faith also Sara herself received strength to conceive seed, and was delivered of a child when she was past age, because she judged him faithful who had promised*" (Heb. 11:11). When it comes to bringing forth the baby, the Scriptures do not refer to a man; they refer to a womb-man.

Sarah needed strength to conceive seed when she was past childbearing age. God met her need. She believed that He was capable of giving her a child regardless of what the circumstances looked like. From a natural perspective, it was impossible. The enemy certainly didn't want it to happen. God, however, performed His promise.

Why would you allow your vision to be incapacitated for the lack of a man? Many women have unbelieving husbands at home. Have faith for yourself. Be a womb-man. It doesn't matter whether someone else believes or not; you cling to the truth that He is doing a good work in you. Each of us needs our own walk with God. Stand back and thank God. Believe God and know that He is able to do it. Sarah didn't stand on her husband's faith; she stood on her own.

You are God's woman. You are not called to sit by the window waiting for God to send you a husband. You had better have some faith yourself and believe God down in your own spirit. If you would believe God, He would perform His Word in your life. No matter the desire or the blessing that you seek, God has promised to give you the desires of your heart (see Ps. 37:4).

Recognize that where life has seemed irrational and out of control, He will turn it around. When trouble was breaking loose in my life and I thought I couldn't take it anymore, God intervened and broke every chain that held me back. He will do no less for you.

YOUR HEALING JOURNEY

You don't need anyone else to see your divine purpose come to pass. Even the people God brings into your life are part of His strategic, divine orchestration.

Sometimes, we look to the left and to the right, thinking that this person, this boyfriend, this husband, this employer, this friend is the key to stepping into our destiny. We mistakenly think that a person has the power to bring us to our next level.

Is this possible? Yes, but only when the person is being directly used by God to do this. It's not wrong for you to believe God for divine connections. It is problematic to trust in the divine connections more than you trust in the Divine Connector.

Day Forty-Six

YOUR PROMISE OF MULTIPLICATION

Blessing I will bless you, and multiplying I will multiply your descendants as the stars of the heaven and as the sand which is on the seashore.
—GENESIS 22:17, NKJV

Abraham had many promises from God regarding his descendants. God told Abraham that his seed would be as the sands of the sea and the stars of Heaven. There were two promises of seed given to Abraham. God said his seed would be as the sands of the earth. That promise represents the natural, physical nation of Israel. These were the people of the Old Covenant.

However, God didn't stop there. He also promised that Abraham's seed would be as the stars of Heaven. These are the people of the New Covenant, the exalted people. That's the Church. We are exalted in Christ Jesus. We too are the seed of Abraham. We are the stars of Heaven.

God had more plans for Abraham's descendants than to simply start a new nation on earth. He planned a new spiritual Kingdom that will last forever. The plan started as a seed, but it ended up as stars.

The only thing between the seed and the stars was the woman. Can you see why Sarah herself had to receive strength to conceive a seed when she was past childbearing age? Because the old man gave her a seed, she gave him the stars of Heaven. Whatever God gives you, He wants it to be multiplied in the womb of your spirit.

When you bring it forth, it shall be greater than the former.

YOUR HEALING JOURNEY

God has dreams for you that are far beyond your ability to grasp or imagine. In order to step into God's dream and see Heaven's purpose brought forth in your life you need to do one thing—surrender.

When you surrender to God, don't look at it as giving "something up." This tends to be the perspective that is emphasized the most. We give up sins, habits, and bad relationships. We give up old practices, destructive ways, and addictions. When this is the emphasis, we always feel like we're giving something up, but we are not living mindful of what Heaven gives us in return.

Don't simply focus on giving something up. With God, surrender is all about making an exchange. You are trading what you have for what He has. You are trading your dream for His dream. At the day's end, the trade-off always seems unfair, not because you are giving so much away, but because you will get so much in return!

OVERCOMING THE ENEMY'S GREAT STRATEGY: FEAR

*For God hath not given us the spirit of fear; but
of power, and of love, and of a sound mind.*
—2 TIMOTHY 1:7

The enemy wants to multiply fear in your life. He wants you
to become so afraid that you won't be able to figure out what
you fear. You may be frightened to live in your own home.
Some are afraid to correct their children. Some people fear
standing up in front of others. Intimidated and afraid, many
do not deliver a prophecy. God wants to set you free from
fear as you are filled with faith.

In order to move forward, we must be willing to give up
yesterday and go on toward tomorrow. We have to trust God
enough to allow Him to come in and plow up our lives. Perhaps He needs to root out closet skeletons and replace them
with new attitudes.

Sometimes women are so accustomed to being hurt that
if anyone comes near them, they become defensive. Some

may look tough and angry toward men, but God knows that behind that tough act they are simply afraid. God deals directly with the issues of the heart and lets you know you do not have to be afraid. The plans of God are good. He is not like the people who have hurt and abused you. He wants only to help you be completely restored.

The enemy chains us to the circumstances of the past to keep us from reaching our potential. Satan has assigned fear to block up your womb. It blocks up your womb and causes you to be less productive than you like. He wants to destroy the spirit of creativity within you.

God wants you to know that you have nothing to fear. You can be creative. He will make you into the womb-man He wants you to be.

Maybe you have been tormented and in pain. You have been upset. You have been frustrated. It is hindering your walk. God is releasing you from fear.

You need to allow Him an opportunity in your life. Then you will start seeing beauty at all different stages of your life. Maybe you have been afraid of aging. God will give you the strength to thank Him for every year.

YOUR HEALING JOURNEY

Fear is a paralyzing spirit that seeks to restrain you from moving forward in life. Fear cripples you from fulfilling God's plan because it forces you to become more mindful of what could/might happen (go wrong) than what God has said. This is why the Israelites wandered in the wilderness for 40 years. They incorrectly measured God beside their fear.

Does this describe you today? Do you see your fears as bigger than God's promises? If so, it's time to break your agreement with the spirit of fear and ask God to give you a greater vision of who He is. We don't overcome fear by simply praying it away. Prayer helps, but we need to replace fear with faith.

How are we expected to have faith to cast out fear and step into the purposes God has for us? Simple. Live grounded in the love of God. He loves you. He's for you. He's equipped you to succeed. He's graced you to win.

Scripture does not tell us that the opposite of fear is faith. In order to have the faith that overcomes fear, we need to have a revelation of God's extravagant, perfect love for us. Remember what John the Apostle wrote, *"perfect love drives out fear"* (1 John 4:18 NIV). When you know how perfectly and completely God loves you, fear may try to come against you, but it will not prevail. Why? Because every promise of God is reinforced by the timeless truth that He loves you. If He loves you, He will bring His purposes to pass in your life—and no enemy or opponent can thwart this from coming to pass!

THE BREAKTHROUGH POWER OF THANKSGIVING

*Enter into His gates with thanksgiving,
and into His courts with praise. Be
thankful to Him, and bless His name.*
—PSALM 100:4, NKJV

Although we must be careful not to become trapped by the past, we should look back and thank God for how He has kept us through the struggles. If you're like me, you will want to say, "I would never have made it if You had not brought me through." Celebrate who you have become through His assistance. In every circumstance, rejoice that He was with you in it.

I believe God is bringing health into dry bones, bones that were bowed over, bones that were bent out of shape, bones that made you upset with yourself. All are giving way to the life of the Spirit. Perhaps you responded to your history with low self-esteem. God will heal the inner wound and teach you how important you are to Him. You do make a difference.

The world would be a different place if it were not for you. You are a part of His divine plan.

When the angel came to Mary and told her what God was going to do in her life, Mary questioned how it could be possible (see Luke 1:34). Perhaps God has been telling you things He wants to do in your life, but you have questioned Him. Perhaps your circumstance does not seem to allow you to accomplish much. Maybe you lack the strength to accomplish the task alone. Perhaps, like Mary, you are thinking only in the natural and that you must have a man to do God's will.

> *And the angel answered and said unto her, The Holy Ghost shall come upon thee, and the power of the Highest shall overshadow thee: therefore also that holy thing which shall be born of thee shall be called the Son of God* (Luke 1:35).

If you have been wondering how God will make things come to pass in your life, remember that He will accomplish the task. No man will get the credit for your deliverance. He told Mary, "*The Holy Ghost shall come upon thee.*" I believe the same is true of godly women today. The Holy Spirit will fill you. He will impregnate you. He will give life to your spirit. He will put purpose back into you. He will renew you. He will restore you.

God had a special plan for Mary. She brought forth Jesus. He has a special plan for us. We, however, aren't privileged to see the future. We don't know what kind of good things He has in store for us. But He has a plan. God's women are to be womb-men. They are to be creative and bring forth new life. That is exactly what God wants to do with those who are broken and discouraged.

YOUR HEALING JOURNEY

Did Mary (the mother of Jesus) experience fear after receiving her divine call from the angel Gabriel? Certainly. But her response was unique. She magnified God. She offered thanksgiving to God, reminding herself of who He was. She recited the great things He had done, giving voice to them in her song of praise (known as the Magnificat).

Even though the life that Mary gave birth to is absolutely unparalleled—the Lord Jesus Christ—God has also called you to give birth to His purposes in the earth. This is one of the reasons you are reading this book and going on this healing journey.

Don't let the enemy tell you that you are second class because you are going through a healing or restoration process. He likes to convince people that they are second-rate because they have "been through it." It's almost like because you've gone through the fire, you somehow become so badly burned that you should not expect to fully be used by God. Maybe half-used, if you're lucky. Maybe just make it through your time on earth and reach the pearly gates… one day.

Do you know why the enemy does this? He's scared—absolutely terrified—of women rising up and giving birth to Heaven's purposes. He's terrified of you becoming like Mary, carrying a promise to full term. He's intimidated by your past. Even though he's tried to intimidate you using your past, use it against him. Turn the tables on the devil. Every ounce of pain you experienced becomes praise. Every trial you went through becomes a testimony that helps usher other women into the place of breakthrough.

Your solution? Give thanks. In all things, give thanks. In spite of your past, give thanks. Regardless of what you're going through right now, give thanks. What do you give thanks for? The fact that God redeems time and redeems hurt. Nothing you've gone through will return void, for the Redeemer will turn it around—not just for your good, but to give you a weapon of testimony that will wreak havoc on the enemy's camp!

Day Forty-Nine

YOUR "YES" IS POWERFUL

Submit yourselves, then, to God. Resist
the devil, and he will flee from you.
—JAMES 4:7, NIV

If great things came from those who never suffered, we might think that they accomplished those things of their own accord. When a broken person submits to God, God gets the glory for the wonderful things He accomplishes—no matter how far that person has fallen. The anointing of God will restore you and make you accomplish great and noble things. Believe it!

The hidden Christ that's been locked up behind your fears, your problems, and your insecurity will come forth in your life. You will see the power of the Lord Jesus do a mighty thing.

After the angel told Mary those words, do you know what she said? *"And Mary said, Behold the handmaid of the Lord; be it unto me according to thy word. And the angel departed from her"* (Luke 1:38). "Be it unto me according to thy word." Not according to my marital status. Not according to my job. Not according to what I deserve. *"Be it unto me according to thy word."*

Mary knew enough to believe God and to submit to Him. She was taking an extreme risk. To be pregnant and unmarried brought dire consequences in those days. Yet she willingly gave herself over to the Lord.

YOUR HEALING JOURNEY

Mary submitted to God by saying a costly but glorious "Yes." She said "Yes" to reproach, to shame, and to being treated as the mother of an illegitimate child. She said "Yes" to a call that didn't make much sense to her human mind, but one that brought joy to the deepest parts of her heart.

What is God asking you to do? Where is He asking for your "Yes"?

Right now, He is bringing you through a healing process. The wonderful thing about the restorative power of God is that it's all about exceeding original condition. Wherever you were before you were hurt—God's not bringing you back to that same place. So many people get discouraged with the healing process because they want everything to go back to "normal." Unfortunately, there are many things that happen to us in life that redefine normal. There will never be a normal like there once was. This is not bad news! God doesn't want you to return to an old way of life because He wants to bring you into a wider space. He wants to amplify what life looks like for you!

The key to participating in God's processes is saying "Yes." When it doesn't make sense. When our results don't come at fast-food speed. When the process seems like it's taking longer than it should. When we're not seeing breakthrough like we thought. When our prayers are not being answered according to our timetable. The devil uses thoughts like this to discourage you from continuing in the healing process. He wants you to cancel the work that God is doing in your life. Don't allow it! God is doing a work in you right now—otherwise, you would not be reading these words.

Even if you have unanswered questions and points of frustration, give God your "Yes." Stick with Him. He's worth it. He's trustworthy!

UNLOCK YOUR FULL POTENTIAL

*And it happened, when Elizabeth heard the
greeting of Mary, that the babe leaped in her womb;
and Elizabeth was filled with the Holy Spirit.*
—LUKE 1:41, NKJV

Mary had a cousin named Elisabeth who was already expecting a child. The child in Elisabeth's womb was to be the forerunner of the Messiah. The two women came together to share their stories. When Elisabeth found a woman who would build her up, the Bible says that the baby leaped in her womb and she was filled with the Holy Ghost.

The things you had stopped believing God for will start leaping in your spirit again. God will renew you. Often women have been working against each other, but God will bring you together. You will come together like Mary and Elisabeth. You will cause your babies to leap in your womb, and the power of the Lord Jesus will do a new thing in your life. The Holy Ghost will come upon you and restore you.

If you are a woman who has had a dream and sensed a promise, reach out to Him. Every woman who knows that they have another woman inside them who hasn't come forth can reach their hearts toward God and He will meet those inner needs and cause them to live at their potential. He will restore what was stolen by your suffering and abuse. He will take back from the enemy what was swallowed up in your history.

He wants to bring you together, sisters. Every Mary needs an Elisabeth. He needs to bring you together. Stop your wars and fighting. Drop your guns. Throw down your swords. Put away your shields. God put something in your sister that you need. When you come together, powerful things will happen.

Satan attempts to keep us from our potential. He allows and causes horrible things to happen in lives so those lives will take on a different outlook. The fear of abuse can be removed only by the power of the Holy Spirit. There is great potential in women who believe. That potential may be locked up at times because of ruined histories. God will wipe the slate clean. He will likely use others to help in the process, but it is His anointing that will bring forth new life from deep within.

YOUR HEALING JOURNEY

To get to the next level in life, you need to surround yourself with people who call out your full potential. This is more important than we realize, as other people often have the ability to see what we don't see. In turn, they are able to call forth the unseen things in our lives, summoning the potential within us.

Additionally, these kind of people can become like Elisabeths to us—just as Elisabeth was to Mary, the mother of Jesus. Mary was pregnant with something impossible. She received a vision. Mary had a divine calling that most people surely rejected as fanatical, imagined, or absolutely ridiculous—"teenage girl impregnated by the Holy Spirit with the Messiah." We cannot imagine that kind of discouragement she received from all ends—even those who were closest to her. This is why her cousin, Elisabeth, was such a blessing to her. Could you imagine what Mary would do if she didn't have Elisabeth? God prepared that woman for such a time and for such a purpose for Mary.

Find your Elisabeth. Find the women who have purpose burning within then. Find those who have also become "pregnant" with the promises of God. They know how to declare. They know how to encourage. They know how to fight on their knees. They know how to press through dry seasons. They know all of this because they too have been filled with an impossible call. These are the voices you need speaking over you in this season of healing!

SET FREE FROM BEING "BOWED OVER"

And he was teaching in one of the synagogues on the
sabbath. And, behold, there was a woman which
had a spirit of infirmity eighteen years, and was
bowed together, and could in no wise lift up herself.
—LUKE 13:10-11

Can you imagine how hard life was for that woman who was bowed over? She had to struggle, because of her problem, to come to Jesus. Few of us are crippled in the same way. However, we all face crippling limitations.

We can be bowed over financially. We can be bowed over emotionally. We can be bowed over where we have no self-esteem. He wants to see us struggling toward Him. Jesus could have walked to this woman, but He chose not to. He wants to see us struggle toward Him.

He wants you to want Him enough to overcome obstacles and to push in His direction. He doesn't want to just throw things at you that you don't have a real conviction to receive.

When you see a humped-over person crawling through the crowd, know that that person really wants help. That kind of desire is what it takes to change your life. Jesus is the answer.

I may seek help by going from one person to another, but only He is the answer. I may be sick in my body, but He is the answer. If my son is dead, or insane on drugs, and I need Him to resurrect my child, He is the answer. If I am having family problems with my brother who is in trouble, He's the answer. It doesn't matter what the problem is, He is the answer.

YOUR HEALING JOURNEY

The Lord wants to bring freedom to every area of your life. Do not compartmentalize His involvement.

So many live their lives without experiencing break-through and victory, not because of God's willingness to give it, but because of their unwillingness to let God into the "everyday." No matter what the problem is, He is the solution.

The woman in Luke 13 was "bowed over" in a crippling way. What areas in your life have been "bowed over"? What areas have been under, not over? What areas have been imprisoned? Think about it. And then come to the Lord in prayer and ask if there are any areas in your life that you have been holding back from God.

Even though this is not always the case, it is frequent. People struggle in areas they are not willing to completely surrender to God. Do not continue this destructive cycle. He desires to have influence in every area of your life so that you can experience His freedom in these areas! God doesn't want to control you; He wants to complete you!

Day Fifty-Two

BREAK THE CYCLES!

*Therefore, since we are surrounded by so great a
cloud of witnesses [who by faith have testified to the
truth of God's absolute faithfulness], stripping off
every unnecessary weight and the sin which so easily
and cleverly entangles us, let us run with endurance
and active persistence the race that is set before us.*
—HEBREWS 12:1, AMP

Most likely your words have hindered you. Often we are
snared by the words in our own mouth. The enemy would
love to destroy you with your own words. Satan has turned
your back against you. He will use your strength against you.
Many of you have beat yourself down with the power of your
own words. You have twisted your own back. The enemy
worked you against yourself until you saw yourself as crippled.
Reverse his plan. If you had enough force to bend yourself,
you've got enough force to straighten yourself back up again.

The Lord told this woman the truth about herself. He told
her that she was loosed and set free. He saw the truth despite
what everyone else saw. She was important.

The religious critics didn't like what Jesus had done. His power showed how powerless their religion was. They accused Him of breaking the law by performing a miracle on the Sabbath day. Christ acknowledged their hypocrisy by addressing a common occurrence in the area. They all valued their livestock, He said. Then He reminded them that they would loose their ass on the Sabbath so that it could get a drink. Surely this woman was more valuable than any animal. She could be loosed from her pain and sickness regardless of the day.

Sometimes pain can become too familiar. Ungodly relationships often become familiar. Change doesn't come easily. Habits and patterns are hard to break. Sometimes we maintain these relationships because we fear change. However, when we see our value the way Jesus sees us, we muster the courage to break away.

He is your defense. He will defend you before your critics. Now is the time for you to focus on receiving the miraculous and getting the water that you could not get before. He is loosing you to water. You haven't been drinking for 18 years, but now you can get a drink. With Jesus, you can do it.

YOUR HEALING JOURNEY

Now that you are willing to give God unrestricted, all-access entrance into your life, ask Him, "Lord, what are some of the unhealthy cycles and patterns in my life?"

Remember, God reveals what He wants to heal. He doesn't bring things up to make you feel guilt, shame, condemnation, self-loathing, etc. This is the work of the enemy. When God reveals through the conviction of the Holy Spirit, it is always for your betterment. He wants you free so you can drink from the waters of life that truly satisfy. Destructive cycles and harmful patterns only perpetuate the enemy's agenda for you. He wants to keep you trapped, when in fact the Scripture clearly says that you have the ability to fix your eyes on Jesus, move in His direction, and strip off every weight that is holding you back.

Return to the Scripture verse at the beginning of this entry—Hebrews 12:1. It doesn't imply that God strips off the unnecessary weights and sins. Rather, it suggests that we have the ability to do this. You, a woman filled with the power of the Holy Spirit, have the ability to break every cycle that you find yourself in.

How do you begin? Ask God for a strategy. Ask the Holy Spirit to lead you. If there are patterns that you find yourself stuck in, target these areas. The Lord might direct you to receive counsel. He may direct you to stop visiting a certain place or spending time with a specific person. He may highlight key activities that He would like you to stop participating in. Please know, God is not trying to "kill your fun." He wants to give you a divine blueprint for breaking out of cycles that have kept you "bowed over" for as long as you can remember. Cooperate with Him in this process. His desire is not to retrain you—it's to release you!

MAKE THE LORD YOUR DESIRE

The Lord is my light and my salvation; whom shall I fear? the Lord is the strength of my life; of whom shall I be afraid? When the wicked, even mine enemies and my foes, came upon me to eat up my flesh, they stumbled and fell. Though an host should encamp against me, my heart shall not fear: though war should rise against me, in this will I be confident. One thing have I desired of the Lord, that will I seek after; that I may dwell in the house of the Lord all the days of my life, to behold the beauty of the Lord, and to enquire in His temple.
—PSALM 27:1-4

You must reach the point where it is the Lord whom you desire. Singleness of heart will bring about deliverance. Perhaps you have spent all your time and effort trying to prove yourself to someone who is gone. Maybe an old lover left you with scars. The person may be dead and buried, but you are still trying to win his approval.

In this case, you are dedicated to worthless tasks. You are committed to things, unattainable goals, that will not satisfy. Christ must be your ambition.

Luke 13:13 reads, *"And immediately she was made straight, and glorified God."* Christ dealt with 18 years of torment in an instant. One moment with Jesus, and immediately she was well. For some things you don't have time to recover gradually. The moment you get the truth, you are loosed. Immediately she recovered.

Once you realize that you have been unleashed, you will feel a sudden change. When you come to Jesus, He will motivate you. You will see that other woman in you. You need to blossom and bring her forth.

YOUR HEALING JOURNEY

The key to working with God to break the cycles in your life is simple—desire God above all else. Make this your prayer. May the cry of David in Psalm 27 reflect your heart's desire as well.

It doesn't mean that we sit in a room all day simply satisfied by God. It doesn't mean we need to cut off all contact with the outside world and go into a life of religious seclusion. What it does mean is that everything and everyone we come into contact with on an everyday basis pales in comparison to the One who satisfies the cry of our soul. This prevents us from getting into harmful soul ties. Our soul is literally tied to the Lover of our soul. The only influences we allow into our lives will be those that cultivate our desire for Him; if they hinder or threaten it, we cannot allow ourselves to become entangled.

When God is your chief desire, every other lesser desire becomes measured next to Him. You find yourself evaluating your desires by whether or not they reflect God.

When your desire for God exceeds any other desire, you have positioned yourself to receive and sustain freedom in your life. The heart that is united to God, desperate for Him above all else, is a heart that will not allow itself to become ensnared by that which leads to bondage. Why? God literally transforms the DNA of your desires. When He is your desire, your desires will reflect His nature. And nothing about Him speaks of bondage!

Day Fifty-Four

YOUR FAITH WILL CHANGE
YOUR CONDITION

*And ought not this woman, being a
daughter of Abraham, whom Satan hath
bound, lo, these eighteen years, be loosed
from this bond on the sabbath day?*
—LUKE 13:16

Jesus called the woman "a daughter of Abraham." She may
have been bent over, but she was still Abraham's daughter.
Don't let your condition negate your position.

She was unleashed because of who her father was. It had
little to do with who she was. The Bible doesn't even mention
her name. We will never know who she was until we reach
Heaven. Although we don't know who she was, we know
whose she was. She was a daughter of Abraham.

Faith is an equal opportunity business. There is no discrimination in it. Faith will work for you. When you approach
God, don't worry about the fact that you are a woman. Never
become discouraged on that basis when it comes to seeking

Him. You will only get as much from God as you can believe Him for.

You won't be able to convince Him, seduce Him, break Him down, or trick Him. God will not move because you cry and act melancholy. Now, you may move me like that. Certainly that works with men, but not with God. God only accepts faith, not just feminine rhetoric, not hysteria—just plain old faith in God.

He wants you to believe Him. He wants you to personalize the truth that you can do all things through Him (see Phil. 4:13). He is trying to teach you so when the time for a real miracle does come, you'll have some faith to draw from. God wants you to understand that if you can believe Him, you can go from defeat to victory and from poverty to prosperity!

YOUR HEALING JOURNEY

Faith is an action that responds to who God is and what God says. This is the foundation for faith. Consider what happened in this part of the story. Jesus calls the woman a daughter of Abraham. He makes a power announcement over her, declaring that her condition does not need to define her position.

When we start identifying ourselves by our condition, it becomes difficult to put faith into action. The woman in this story may have identified herself by her crippling condition. The woman with the "issue of the blood" could have easily identified herself by her condition. Blind Bartimaeus could have identified himself by his condition. They did not. This is the key to their victory and why they were able to activate faith.

When you see your condition as your position, your malady as your identity, you end up defining yourself by something that God wants to remove from your life. It may be crippling. It may be eating away at you. It may be destroying your life. It may be robbing you of sleep. You know it's harmful, but you never envisioned a reality where you were not experiencing the pain of your problem. It's gone on for so long that, perhaps, you fear a world without it—not because you enjoy the pain, but because you would not know how to live as a free woman.

Right now, I declare—just like Jesus did to the woman who was "bowed over" in Luke 13—that you are a daughter of God! You are seated with Christ Jesus in the heavenly places. You are a joint heir with the Son of God. You were fashioned for greatness. You need to see yourself as God sees you, and as you do, it doesn't matter how long you have experienced your condition, you know it's time for a change. You know that He wants to loose you and let you go!

This fact gives you the ability to put your faith to action. When you know what God has said about you, you become discontent living in a world of contradiction. You don't want to live out of alignment with how Heaven sees you. "The Word of God says I'm the head and not the tail... but right now, I feel completely overwhelmed. I feel like the tail. I feel bowed over. This is not God's will, so I am going to believe Him. I'm going to start walking and talking and living like I'm above and not beneath, in Jesus's Name!"

Day Fifty-Five

PUT YOUR FAITH TO WORK

Faith without works is dead.
—JAMES 2:20, NKJV

Faith is more than a fact—faith is an action. Don't tell me you believe when your actions do not correspond with your conviction. If your actions don't change, you might still think you are tied. When you finally understand that you are loose, you will start behaving as if you were set free.

When you are loose, you can go anywhere. If I had one end of a rope around my neck, I would only be able to walk the length of the rope. Once I am unleashed from that rope, I can walk as far as I want. You are whole; you are loose. You can go anywhere.

Hebrews chapter 11 is a faith "hall of fame." It lists great people of God who believed Him and accomplished great exploits. Abraham is given tremendous attention in this chapter. He is revered by millions as the father of faith. He is the first man in history to believe God to the point where it was counted as righteousness. He was saved by faith. Jesus said that the infirm woman was a daughter of Abraham. She was worthy. She had merit because she was Abraham's descendant and had faith.

There are two contrasting women mentioned in the faith "hall of fame." Sarah, Abraham's wife, is listed. Rahab, the Jericho prostitute, is listed as well. A married woman and a whore made it to the hall of fame. A good, clean, godly woman and a whore made it into the book. I understand how Sarah was included, but how in the world did this prostitute get to be honored? She was listed because God does not honor morality. He honors faith. That was the one thing they had in common; nothing else.

The Bible doesn't talk about Rahab having a husband. She had the whole city. Sarah stayed in the tent and knit socks. She moved wherever her husband went and took care of him. There was no similarity in their lifestyles, just in their faith. God saw something in Sarah that He also saw in Rahab. Do not accept the excuse that because you have lived like a Rahab you can't have the faith experience.

God wants you to believe Him. Make a decision and stand on it. Rahab decided to take a stand on the side of God's people. She hid the spies. She made the decision based on her faith. She took action. Faith is a fact and faith is an action. She took action because she believed God would deliver her when Jericho fell to the Israelites.

YOUR HEALING JOURNEY

What do all of the heroes and heroines of the faith have in common? They acted on what they believed. Even to receive Jesus as your Lord and Savior, you need to take a step of faith. You receive His redemptive work on the Cross and invite Him into your heart. There are steps to faith. There are actions that precede breakthrough.

How much do you want to be free? Your desire to experience the fullness of God's promises in your life will determine whether or not you put your faith to work. The desire must consume you. No longer is freedom something to be grasped; it's your identity in Christ. You may not look free or feel free right now, but the Word of God declares that if Jesus Christ has set you free, then you are free indeed! (See John 8:36.)

Now it's time to start living out what has already been declared in Scripture. If you are identified by Jesus Himself "free indeed," don't accept anything in your life that prevents this freedom from manifesting. The forces that threaten your freedom should become the target of your prayers of faith! According to Scripture, it's not enough to simply say "I have faith." True faith comes with a demonstration. True faith compels you to action. Anything less is a counterfeit of faith. Perhaps it's "wishing and hoping," but it's not Bible faith.

Remember, you are not saved by your works. It's your faith in God's grace. Period. And yet, in order to access the grace of God for salvation, you need to act. You need to believe something and start living like that belief is actually your new reality!

Day Fifty-Six

FAITH IS NO RESPECTER OF PERSONS

By faith Sarah herself also received strength
to conceive seed, and she bore a child when
she was past the age, because she judged
Him faithful who had promised.
—HEBREWS 11:11, NKJV

Sarah received strength to carry and deliver a child when she was well past childbearing age. She took action because she judged Him faithful who had promised. She went through the birth process and delivered a child not because of her circumstance, but because of her faith. She believed God.

God wants your faith to be developed. Regardless of your position and your past, God raises people up equally. Faith is an equal opportunity business. No matter how many mistakes you have made, it is still faith that God honors. You see, you may have blown it, but God is in the business of restoring broken lives. You may have been like Rahab, but if you can believe God, He will save your house. You know, He didn't save only her. He saved her entire household. All the other homes in Jericho were destroyed. The only house God saved in the city was the house where the prostitute lived.

You would have thought He would have saved some nice little lady's house. Perhaps He would have saved some cottage housing an old woman, or a little widow's house, with petunias growing on the sidewalk. No, God saved the whore's house. Was it because He wanted it? No, He wanted the faith. That is what moves God.

If you believe that your background will keep you from moving forward with God, then you don't understand the value of faith. The thing God is asking from you is faith. Some may live good, clean, separated lives; maybe you are proud of how holy you are. He still honors only faith.

If you want to grasp the things of God, you will not be able to purely because of your lifestyle, but because of your conviction. God gave healing to some folks who weren't even saved. They were sinners. Perhaps some of them never did get saved, but they got healed because they believed Him. The thing that moves God is faith. If you believe Him, He will move in your life according to your faith and not your experience.

YOUR HEALING JOURNEY

Faith levels the playing field. It doesn't matter where you came from—it only matters that you believe God. Simple as that. Believe Him. Rely upon Him. Trust His goodness and His character. He will not fail you. He will not let you down. He will not pull the rug out from under you.

While reading, you might have some hesitation about going "all in" with God. Perhaps you're concerned that your history will keep you from God's destiny for you. Maybe He'll save you from your sins and prepare a place for you in Heaven...but on earth, you'll just have to "make it by." The devil is a liar! God did not redeem you with the precious blood of His Son and fill you with Heaven's treasure, the Holy Spirit, so you could sleepwalk through life.

Have faith. No matter where you came from or what you came out of, God is bigger than your past. Believe Him. Cling to His promises. Trust Him wholeheartedly. This is what truly pleases God.

REMIND THE DEVIL OF WHOSE DAUGHTER YOU ARE

Then came the daughters of Zelophehad, the son of
Hepher, the son of Gilead, the son of Machir, the
son of Manasseh, of the families of Manasseh, the son
of Joseph: and these are the names of his daughters;
Mahlah, Noah, and Hoglah, and Milcah, and Tirzah.
And they stood before Moses, and before Eleazar the
priest, and before the princes and all the congregation,
by the door of the tabernacle of the congregation,
saying, Our father died in the wilderness, and
he was not in the company of them that gathered
themselves together against the Lord in the company
of Korah; but died in his own sin, and had no sons.
—NUMBERS 27:1-3

There was a group of sisters in the Old Testament who proved that God is interested in what happens to women.

They were a group of women who were left alone. There were no men left in the family. Their father had wealth, but he had no sons. Prior to this time, women were not allowed to own property or to have an inheritance except through their husbands. Only men could own property.

They continued with their appeal. *"Why should the name of our father be done away from among his family, because he hath no son? Give unto us therefore a possession among the brethren of our father"* (Num. 27:4).

They appealed to Moses for help on the basis of who their father was. They stated their case and looked to him as God's authority. They couldn't understand why they should not have some of their father's wealth simply because they were born female. Their uncles would have received all their father's wealth. They would have been poor and homeless, receiving only leftovers from others. However, these women were daughters of Abraham.

If you want the enemy to release you, remind him whose daughter you are.

YOUR HEALING JOURNEY

Remind the enemy of whose daughter you are! He wants to blind you to your identity in Christ. As long as he gets you thinking like someone who is in bondage, you will remain in bondage. When you start thinking of yourself as a daughter of God, you will come to the conclusion that bondage has no place in your life!

Day Fifty-Eight

PLACE A DEMAND ON YOUR FAMILY INHERITANCE

And Moses brought their cause before the Lord.
And the Lord spake unto Moses, saying, The
daughters of Zelophehad speak right: thou shalt
surely give them a possession of an inheritance
among their father's brethren; and thou shalt cause
the inheritance of their father to pass unto them.
—NUMBERS 27:5-7

No one would have listened to them if they had not initiated a meeting to plead their case. Perhaps you have struggled to call a meeting. Get in touch with people in power and demand what you want, or you will not get it. Speak for yourself. They could not understand why they were being discriminated against because of their gender.

One of the reasons Zelophehad's daughters could make a proper case for themselves was they were right. It was time to teach God's people that women have value. Abraham's daughters have worth. They didn't wait for a man to defend them; they took action in faith. God saw faith in those women.

In verses 5-7, Moses didn't know what to do, so he asked God. The women were vindicated. If they had failed, surely they would have been scorned by all the good people of Israel who would have never challenged Moses in such a way. Instead, they received the wealth of their father. God is no respecter of persons. Faith is based on equal opportunity.

Like the infirm woman, you are a daughter of Abraham if you have faith. You want the inheritance of your father to pass on to you. Why should you sit there and be in need when your Father has left you everything? Your Father is rich, and He left everything to you. However, you will not get your inheritance until you ask for it. Demand what your Father left you. That degree has your name on it. That promotion has your name on it. That financial breakthrough has your name on it.

There is no need to sit around waiting for someone else to get you what is yours. Nobody else is coming. The One who needed to come has already come. Jesus said, "*I am come that they might have life, and that they might have it more abundantly*" (John 10:10). That is all you need.

YOUR HEALING JOURNEY

Faith cannot be passive; it must be active. In fact, there is often a violence to faith because faith demands. It does not demand from God. In fact, we never order God to do anything; that is not what faith is all about. True faith—rooted in the Word of God and the nature of God—observes that which is not in agreement with His will as hostile to God's purposes. Such hindrances are barriers that need to be removed urgently and with force.

Perhaps this is why Jesus used the specific language He did when talking about faith in Mark 11, telling His audience that even the smallest amount of faith could send mountains into the sea. Faith is your key to receiving the family inheritance as a daughter of the Father. Yes, there is a great inheritance waiting for you. In fact, it's already yours. You simply need to receive it. You need to access it. You need to place a demand on what belongs to you, through faith.

This is how you are able to deal with bondages, adversity, pain, and trials. Cast those mountains into the sea by using your faith!

Day Fifty-Nine

SPEAK LIKE A DAUGHTER WITH AN INHERITANCE

Death and life are in the power of the tongue:
and they that love it shall eat the fruit thereof.
—PROVERBS 18:21

The power to get wealth is in your tongue. You shall have whatever you say. If you keep sitting around murmuring, groaning, and complaining, you use your tongue against yourself. Your speech has got you bent over and crippled. You may be destroying yourself with your words.

Open your mouth and speak something good about yourself so you can stand up on your feet. You used your mouth against yourself. Then you spoke against all the other women around you because you treated them like you treated yourself. Open your mouth now and begin to speak deliverance and power. You are not defeated. You are Abraham's daughter.

When you start speaking correctly, God will give you what you say. You say you want it. Jesus said, *"And all things, whatsoever ye shall ask in prayer, believing, ye shall receive"*

(Matt. 21:22). God willed you something. Your Father left you an inheritance. If God would bless the sons of Abraham, surely He would bless the daughters of Abraham.

God will give you whatever you ask for (see John 14:13). God will give you a business. God will give you a dream. He will make you the head and not the tail (see Deut. 28:13). God's power brings all things up under your feet. Believe Him for your household. God will deliver. You don't need a sugar daddy. You have the Jehovah Jireh, the best provider this world has ever known.

YOUR HEALING JOURNEY

This is not a call to "name it and claim" whatever you want. You are not just speaking any old thing. You're not reciting a positive mantra. You're not thinking happy thoughts. It's so much more powerful than that. To speak in faith is to agree with God, even if circumstances are contrary to what is revealed in His Word. You are not denying reality. You clearly acknowledge the reality of what your circumstances are saying—you just recognize that those circumstances are subject to a higher, more superior reality. This is the reality of Heaven. The reality of God's Word. The reality of God's promises. The reality of what the Maker of Heaven and Earth says about you and your situation!

In the same way that the circumstances of life try to obscure your vision of God, filling your heart with fear and your mind with worry, the enemy is constantly trying to assign a false identity to you. He wants you to agree with his lies about what he thinks about you. You need to remember this. When the devil opens his mouth, he's lying. That's all he does; Jesus called him the father of lies. Don't agree with the descriptions he tries to assign you. Believe that you are God's beloved! You are His chosen daughter! You are redeemed and guilt-free! You are anointed by the Holy Spirit! You were created for greatness! Believe it and speak it forth. May the words of your mouth be the fruit of a heart that's anchored in your identity in Christ.

Day Sixty

YOU ARE NOT SECOND CLASS IN THE KINGDOM OF GOD

For as many of you as have been baptized into Christ have put on Christ. There is neither Jew nor Greek, there is neither bond nor free, there is neither male nor female: for ye are all one in Christ Jesus.
—GALATIANS 3:27-28

Women are just as much children of God as men are. Everything that God will do for a man, He will do for a woman. You are not disadvantaged. You can get an inheritance like any man. Generally men don't cry about being single— they simply get on with life and stay busy. There is no reason a woman can't be complete in God without a husband.

Those ancient Israelite women, the daughters of Zelophehad, thought it was a disgrace for them to be starving when they considered who their father was. Rahab was a harlot until she found faith. Once she had faith, she no longer turned to her old profession. The infirm woman was bowed over until Jesus touched her. Once He touched her, she stood up. You have put on Christ. There is no reason to be bent over after His touch. You can walk with respect even when you have past failures. It's not what people say about you that makes you different. It is what you say about yourself and what your God has said about you that really matters.

Just because someone calls you a tramp doesn't mean you have to act like one. Rahab walked with respect. You will find her name mentioned in the lineage of Jesus Christ. She went from being a prostitute to being one of the great-grandmothers of our Lord and Savior Jesus Christ. You can't help where you've been, but you can help where you're going.

God is not concerned about race. If you are African-American, He is not concerned about you being black. You may think, "My people came over on a boat and picked cotton on a plantation." It doesn't make any difference. The answer isn't to be white. Real spiritual advantage does not come from the color of your skin. It's not the color of your skin that will bring deliverance and help from God; it's the contents of your heart.

Some of us have particular problems based on where we came from. We've got to deal with it. God says there is neither Greek nor Jew. There is no such thing as a black church. There is no such thing as a white church. It's only one Church, purchased by the blood of the Lamb. We are all one in Christ Jesus.

You may have been born with a silver spoon in your mouth too, but it doesn't make any difference. In the Kingdom of

God, social status doesn't mean anything. Rahab can be mentioned right next to Sarah because if you believe, God will bless. Faith is the only thing in this world where there is true equal opportunity. Everyone can come to Jesus.

YOUR HEALING JOURNEY

God doesn't look at your gender; He looks at your heart. He doesn't look at morality and good works. He looks at the faith that lives within. God is looking in your heart. You are spirit, and spirits are sexless. That's why angels don't have sexes; they simply are ministering spirits. Don't think of angels in terms of gender. They can manifest themselves as men in shape or form, but angels are really ministering spirits. All people are one in Christ Jesus.

Christ saw the worth of the infirm woman because she was a daughter of Abraham. She had faith. He will unleash you also from the pain you have struggled with and the frustrations that have plagued you. Faith is truly equal opportunity. If you will but dare to believe that you are a daughter of Abraham, you will find the power to stand up straight and be unleashed. The potential that has been bound will then truly be set free!

HAVING THE ATTITUDE OF CHRIST

Let this mind be in you, which
was also in Christ Jesus.
—PHILIPPIANS 2:5

Attitudes affect the way we live our lives. A good attitude can bring success. A poor attitude can bring destruction. An attitude results from perspective. I'm sure you understand what perspective is. Everyone seems to have a different perspective. It comes from the way we look at life, and the way we look at life is often determined by our history.

The events of the past can cause us to have an outlook or perspective on life that is less than God's perspective. The little girl who was abused learns to defend herself by not trusting men. This attitude of defensiveness often stretches into adulthood. If we have protected ourselves a certain way in the past with some measure of success, then it is natural to continue that pattern throughout life. Unfortunately, we often need to learn how to look past our perspective and change our attitudes.

The infirm woman whom Jesus healed was made completely well by His touch. She couldn't help herself no matter how hard she tried, but Jesus unleashed her. He lifted a heavy burden from her shoulders and set her free.

Today, many of us have things we need to be separated from or burdens we need lifted. We will not function effectively until those things are lifted off of us. We can function to a certain point under a load, but we can't function as effectively as we would if the thing was lifted off of us. Perhaps some of you right now have things that are burdening you down.

You need to commend yourselves for having the strength to function under pressure. Unfortunately, we often bear the weight of it alone because we don't feel free to tell anyone about our struggles. So whatever strides you have made, be they large or small, you have made them against the current.

YOUR HEALING JOURNEY

Over the next few days, we are going to be reviewing one of the most profound changes you can undergo in order to walk in the freedom that Jesus made available to you—an attitude shift!

When you model the attitude of Jesus, you position yourself to experience the life of Jesus. A bad attitude is living out of agreement with God's divine design for you.

You were saved from your sins, not simply to go to Heaven one day, but to reveal what a woman filled with God looks like on the earth.

The world is a dry and weary place. It longs for the living water that is within you. One of the ways to release this living water is to demonstrate the character of Jesus. When people see Jesus in action, they move toward Him. He stirs a hunger in their hearts that pulls them toward His presence. How do you see Jesus revealed in your life?

First thing: commit to modeling His attitude. Think like He does. How do you know how Jesus thinks? Read the Scriptures. They reveal how God thinks—and in turn, how you are supposed to think. Your thoughts determine your attitude. In order to have the attitude of Christ, first you need to have the thought life of Christ.

Ask the Holy Spirit to help you think like Jesus. He is the only One capable of giving you that ability. The wonderful thing is that it is the Father's good pleasure to give that to you!

Day Sixty-Two

A SPIRITUAL IDENTITY CRISIS

And God raised us up with Christ and seated us
with him in the heavenly realms in Christ Jesus.
—EPHESIANS 2:6, NIV

It is God's intention that we be set free from the loads we carry. Many people live in codependent relationships. Others are anesthetized to their problems because they have had them so long. Perhaps you have become so accustomed to having a problem that even when you get a chance to be delivered, you find it hard to let it go. Problems can become like a security blanket.

Jesus took away this woman's excuse. He said, "Woman, thou art loosed from thine infirmity." The moment He said that, it required something of her that she hadn't had to deal with before. For 18 years she could excuse herself because she was handicapped. The moment He told her the problem was gone, she had no excuse.

Before you get out of trouble, you need to straighten out your attitude. Until your attitude is corrected, you can't be corrected.

Why should we put up all the ramps and rails for the handicapped if we can heal them? You want everyone to make an allowance for your problem, but your problem needs to make an allowance for God and to humble itself to the point where you don't need special help. I'm not referring to physical handicaps; I'm addressing the emotional baggage that keeps us from total health. You cannot expect the whole human race to move over because you had a bad childhood. They will not do it. So you will end up in depression and frustration and even confusion. You may have trouble with relationships because people don't accommodate your hang-up.

One woman I pastored was extremely obnoxious. It troubled me deeply, so I took the matter to God in prayer. The Lord allowed me to meet her husband. When I saw how nasty he talked to her, I understood why—when she reached down into her reservoir, all she had was hostility. That's all she had taken in. You cannot give out something that you haven't taken in.

Christ wants to separate you from the source of your bitterness until it no longer gives you the kind of attitude that makes you a carrier of pain. Your attitude affects your situation—your attitude, not other people's attitude about you. Your attitude will give you life or death.

YOUR HEALING JOURNEY

It's time to change the way you see yourself. In order to move further into your journey of healing and full restoration, you need to stop identifying yourself by your malady, your past, your pain, your problem, your issue, and instead identify yourself by your position in Christ. Scripture says you are seated with Jesus in the heavenly places.

Stop defining yourself by the "low places" you've been in—or that you are currently getting delivered from. See yourself seated with Christ in heavenly places. Let this thought dominate you when it comes to your concept of personal identity. You may not be walking that out fully, but that is your objective. That is your great quest. To see your life down here (on earth) model the life you already have in Christ up there (in Heaven).

Day Sixty-Three

GET YOUR ATTITUDE DELIVERED!

And be not conformed to this world: but be ye transformed by the renewing of your mind.
—ROMANS 12:2

One of the greatest deliverances people can ever experience in life is to have their attitude delivered. It doesn't do you any good to be delivered financially if your attitude doesn't change. I can give you five thousand dollars, but if your attitude, your mental perspective, doesn't change, you will be broke in a week because you'll lose it again. The problem is not how much you have, it's what you do with what you have. If you can change your attitude, you might have only fifty dollars, but you'll take that fifty and learn how to get five million.

When God comes to heal, He wants to heal your emotions also. Sometimes all we pray about is our situation. We bring God our shopping list of desires. Fixing circumstances is like applying a Band-Aid, though. Healing attitudes sets people free to receive wholeness.

The woman who was crippled for 18 years was delivered from her infirmity. The Bible says she was made straight and glorified God. She got a new attitude. However, the enemy still tried to defeat her by using the people around her. He does not want to let you find health and strength. He may send another circumstance that will pull you down in the same way if you don't change your attitude.

When you first read about this woman, you might have thought that the greatest deliverance was her physical deliverance. I want to point out another deliverance that was even greater. The Bible said that when the Lord laid His hand on her, she was made straight. That's physical deliverance. Then her attitude changed. She entered into praise and thanksgiving and worshiped the Lord. This woman began to leap and rejoice and magnify God and shout the victory like anybody who has been delivered from an 18-year infirmity should. While she was glorifying God over here, the enemy was stirring up strife over there. She just kept on glorifying God. She didn't stop praising God to answer the accusers.

YOUR HEALING JOURNEY

Ask the Lord today for an attitude deliverance. You might think, "I don't need that!" We all do. Deliverance is part of sanctification, and sanctification is the process of putting off the old and putting on the new.

What does this all mean? Your old life, before you met Christ, is tainted in many ways by perspectives, attitudes, and habits. Even though our spirit is instantly transformed by the Holy Spirit, it doesn't take long before we see how much help our body needs to get caught up with our redeemed spirit. It's a lifelong process. It's not about some kind of holiness "to do" check-off list. It's about asking God to supernaturally transform you from the inside out. One of the key places that deliverance begins is in the attitude—especially for those who have painful pasts.

Right now, invite the Holy Spirit to come and lead you through the deliverance process. It's not spooky. It's not weird. It's part of growing up in the Lord. The goal? That you would have the same attitude that was in Christ Jesus—that your attitude would model His. Don't expect anything instant. Again, it's a lifelong process that we need to begin in order to experience the full, abundant life Jesus made available to us!

Day Sixty-Four

ENTER INTO DEFENSIVE PRAISE

*Immediately she was made straight,
and glorified God.*
—LUKE 13:13

The Lord is your defense. You do not have to defend yourself. When God has delivered you, do not stop what you're doing to answer your accusers. Continue to bless His name, because you do not want your attitude to become defensive. When you have been through difficult times, you cannot afford to play around with moods and attitudes. Depression and defensiveness may make you vulnerable to the devil.

This woman had to protect herself by entering into defensive praise. This was not just praise of thanksgiving, but defensive praise. Defensive praise is a strategy and a posture of war that says, "We will not allow our attitude to crumble and fall."

When you get to the point that you quit defending yourself or attacking others, you open up a door for the Lord to fight for you.

When this woman began to bless God, she built walls around her own deliverance. She decided to keep the kind of attitude that enabled the deliverance of God to be maintained in her life. When you have been through surgery, you cannot afford to fool around with Band-Aids.

When you're in trouble, God will reach into the mess and pull you out. However, you must be strong enough not to let people drag you back into it. Once God unleashes you, don't let anyone trap you into some religious fight. Keep praising Him. For this woman, the more they criticized her, the more she was justified because she just stood there and kept believing God. God is trying to get you to a place of faith. He is trying to deliver you from an attitude of negatives.

When you have had problems for many years, you tend to expect problems. God must have healed this woman's emotions also because she kept praising Him instead of paying attention to the quarrel of the religious folks around her. She could have easily fallen into negative thinking. Instead, she praised God.

Can you imagine what would have happened if she had stopped glorifying God and started arguing? If an argument could have gotten through her doors, this whole scene would have ended in a fight. But she was thankful and determined to express her gratitude.

YOUR HEALING JOURNEY

As you go through the healing process, choose to praise as your defense. Remember, you have an enemy who will be fighting you along the journey. He will ever seek to bring you into the prison of condemnation, where you become overwhelmed by everything that needs fixing. Don't go there. You're on a journey and praise God every day for every single step of progress you make. Praise actually reorients your perspective to be mindful of God's work in your life. It elevates your eyes to look upon Him instead of being preoccupied with earthly things. Finally, praise magnifies the Lord.

What does it mean to magnify God through praise? Think of it this way. When it comes to size, God is already infinitely beyond our capacity to grasp. How is it possible for mere human beings to magnify Him—increase God in size? It's not possible. God is big. Period. Here's the question: How big is He to you? Praise brings your vision of God into agreement with what Scripture says about who He is.

ALLOW OTHERS INTO YOUR STORY

*Bear one another's burdens, and
so fulfill the law of Christ.*
—GALATIANS 6:2, ESV

Many couples in a relationship argue over relatively insignificant things. Often the reason these things are important is one or the other is reminded of a past event. How can one person love another if he or she doesn't know the other person's history?

The Church has become too narrow in its approach to attitude. We want to keep our attitudes to ourselves and simply take them to God. Although we certainly should take them to Him, we also need to learn to "*bear ye one another's burdens*" (Gal. 6:2).

Thousands walk in fear. The Church can give strength to counter that fear. Thousands have built a wall around themselves because they do not trust anyone else. The Church can help its members learn to trust one another. Thousands are codependent and get their value from a relationship with another person. The Church can point to God's love as the source for self-worth. We are not valuable because we love God; we are valuable because He loves us.

Jesus took away the ability of the infirm woman to make excuses for herself and gave her the strength to maintain an attitude of gratitude and praise. The Church today is to be the kind of safe haven that does the same thing. Those who are wounded should be able to come and find strength in our praise.

Gratitude and defensive praise are contagious. Although the Bible doesn't specifically say so, I imagine that those who saw what was going on the day Jesus healed the infirm woman were caught up in praise as well. The Church also must find room to join in praise when the broken are healed. Those who missed the great blessing that day were those who decided to argue about religion.

The Bible describes Heaven as a place where the angels rejoice over one sinner who comes into the faith (see Luke 15:10). They rejoice because Jesus heals those who are broken. Likewise God's people are to rejoice because the broken-hearted and emotionally wounded come to Him.

Christ unleashed power in the infirm woman that day. He healed her body and gave her the strength of character to keep a proper attitude. The woman who is broken and wounded today will find power unleashed within her too when she responds to the call and brings her wounds to the Great Physician.

YOUR HEALING JOURNEY

Isolation is not God's solution when we are experiencing healing. In fact, the enemy looks for those who are living in isolation as he knows they are prime targets. When we live in community with other people of like-precious faith, we are able to strengthen one another. As Scripture says, "iron sharpens iron."

In the New Testament, James writes about confessing our sins one to another that we would be healed. There is healing in community. Why? Because in those seasons when we feel absolutely unable to carry our burden, God sends others to help us.

You were never meant to be an island unto yourself. As you walk out this healing journey, find a community that can support and strengthen you every step of the way!

APPRECIATE YOUR BEAUTY

Charm can mislead and beauty soon fades.
The woman to be admired and praised is the
woman who lives in the Fear-of-God.
—PROVERBS 31:30, MSG

We are fascinated with beauty. There are contests of all kinds to determine who is the most beautiful of all. Advertisers spend millions of dollars to promote beauty pageants. The beauty industry is one of the largest in America. Women spend huge amounts of money on makeup, fashionable clothing, and jewelry. Plastic surgeons are kept busy cutting and tucking extra flesh and reshaping features to make people more attractive.

In spite of all this attention, what is the true beauty of a woman? What is it that makes her genuinely attractive? Many feel unattractive because they don't meet a certain image to which they have aspired. Others are constantly frustrated in trying to get someone to notice their attractiveness.

No scientist has ever been able to make a woman. No doctor has been able to create a woman. No engineer has been able to build a woman. However, God has made fine women. You don't have to look like a TV commercial to be beautiful. No one stays 21 forever.

We must learn to thank God for who we are. Don't be a silly woman watching television and crying because she doesn't look like the girl who opened up the window in the game show. You are not supposed to look like that. If God had wanted you to look like that, He would have made you like that. God will send somebody along who will appreciate you the way you are.

Start appreciating yourself. Remind yourself, "I am valuable to God. I am somebody. And I won't let another use me and abuse me and treat me like I'm nothing. Yes, I've been through some bad times. I've been hurt and I've been bent out of shape, but the Lord touched me and loosed me and now I am glorifying God and I'm not going back to where I came from."

YOUR HEALING JOURNEY

You are valuable to God because of who you are. He finds you absolutely breathtaking and beautiful! The Bible says you were fearfully and wonderfully made.

One way you practice the fear of the Lord is believing what He says above all other voices. When we truly revere God, it does not mean we stoically stand back from Him, shuttering in dread. The fear of the Lord produces a new value for His Word. When we awe Him, we awe His Word. When we awe His Word, we consider what He says to be absolutely life-defining for us. So start stepping into a new dimension of the fear of God by believing, wholeheartedly, what He says about you. He sees you as beautiful!

YOUR INNER GLORY

*The Lord does not look at the things
people look at. People look at the outward
appearance, but the Lord looks at the heart.*
—1 SAMUEL 16:7, NIV

There is an important lesson to learn from the account of Samson and Delilah in the Old Testament. The Philistines were Samson's enemies and they could not kill Samson with swords or bows, but they found a door. The Bible says that Samson loved Delilah. He became so infatuated with her that he was vulnerable.

It was not Delilah's beauty that captivated. It was not even her sexuality that destroyed Samson. Samson had known beautiful women before. He had slept with prostitutes. It was not just sexual exercise that caused her to get a grip on this man. I'll call it the Delilah syndrome.

Beauty and sex appeal are not the areas to concentrate on. When you focus on the wrong areas, you don't get the right results. Society teaches you today that if you have the right hair, the right face, the right shape, the right clothes, and the right car, then you will get the right man. Then you can expect that you will buy the right house, have the right children, live the right life, and live happily ever after. That is simply not true. Life is not a fairy tale.

God put some things into the feminine spirit that a man needs more than anything God put on the feminine body. If a woman knows who she is on the inside, no matter what she looks like, she will have no problem being attractive to a man. If she knows her own self-worth, then when she comes before that man, he will receive her.

The enemy wants you to be so focused on your outer appearance that you won't recognize your inner beauty, your inner strength, your inner glory. Your real value cannot be bought, applied, added on, hung from your ears, or laid on your neck. Your real strength is more than outward apparel and adornment for men. This real thing that causes a man to need you so desperately he can't leave you is not what is on you, but what is in you.

You need to recognize what God has put in you. God, when He made the woman, didn't just decorate the outside. He decorated the inside of the woman. He put beauty in her spirit.

YOUR HEALING JOURNEY

Your inner beauty is your inner glory. When this is unleashed, you become a wellspring of life, flourishing in every way. Why aren't more women flourishing in life?

Distraction. They are convinced that the key to "success" and happiness is focusing on external appearance. While it seems like everyone focuses on the outside, God gazes into the innermost parts of your being. He loves what He sees. He sees a spirit that He uniquely crafted. He sees the true you. He sees the beautiful one who was worth every drop of Jesus's blood that was spilled on the Cross of Calvary. Remember that!

THE POWER OF WHAT YOU CARRY ON THE INSIDE

Whose adorning let it not be that outward adorning of plaiting the hair, and of wearing of gold, or of putting on of apparel.
—1 PETER 3:3

If First Peter 3:3 meant you could not wear these things, then it would mean you must be naked. Woman's beauty and strength are not on the outside. There is more to you than clothes. There's more to you than gold. There's more to you than hairstyles. If you keep working only on these outer things, you will find yourself looking in the mirror to find your value.

The Scriptures talk about not having the outward adornment of gold, silver, and costly array. The Church took that passage and made a legal doctrine out of it. It was declared that there could be no jewelry, no makeup, and no clothing of certain types. We are so negative at times. We were so busy dealing with the negative that we didn't hear the positive of what God said. God said that He had adorned the woman inwardly.

Likewise, ye wives, be in subjection to your own husbands (1 Peter 3:1a).

Notice that it didn't say a woman is to be subject to all men, just to her own husband. God did not make you a servant to all men. You have the right to choose who you will be in subjection to—and please choose very carefully.

That, if any obey not the word, they also may without the word be won by the conversation of the wives (1 Peter 3:1b).

Understand that the word *conversation* there refers to lifestyle. You will not win him through lip service; you will win him through your lifestyle. He will see how you are, not what you say. He will watch how you act. He will watch your attitude. He will watch your disposition. A real problem for women believers today is that with the same mouth they use to witness to their husbands, they often curse others. You cannot witness to and win a man while he sits up and listens to you gossip about others.

YOUR HEALING JOURNEY

Let's focus a little more on your inner glory. This is your lifestyle. Your speech. How you carry yourself. All of these things unveil your inner glory. There might be women who are externally "beautiful," but they don't recognize their inner glory. They don't cultivate it and as a result, it does not shine through. "Pretty" does not compensate for inner glory. Unfortunately, many women invest more time in that which is temporary and fading than that which is eternal.

Again, this is because the enemy works overtime to distract women to be more conscious of physical appearance than internal appearance. Why? When women discover who they really are, they become a threat to the works of darkness. When Jesus is revealed, darkness is pushed back. When women start to resemble their Creator and Savior, the very One who conquered the devil at the Cross continues to enforce this victory through the lives of redeemed, victorious, Spirit-filled daughters of God.

They become catalysts for awakening. One awakened woman awakens another to her inner beauty. When the interior becomes the greater emphasis than the exterior, women emerge as daughters of God who cooperate with the Holy Spirit and purpose to look more like Christ rather than being those who want to mirror the latest fashion fad or supermodel.

YOU ARE SARAH'S DAUGHTER

Even as Sara obeyed Abraham, calling him lord:
whose daughters ye are, as long as ye do well,
and are not afraid with any amazement.
—1 PETER 3:6

You are Sarah's daughters when you are not afraid with any amazement. When you resist the temptation to react to circumstances and maintain a peaceful, meek, and quiet spirit in times of frustration, then you are Sarah's daughters.

Jesus called the infirm woman. He unleashed a daughter of Abraham. If you can stay calm in a storm, if you can praise God under pressure, if you can worship in the midst of critics and criticism, God says you are Sarah's daughter.

If you can keep a calm head when the bills are more than the income, and not lose control when satan says you won't make it, if you can stand in the midst of the storm, you are Sarah's daughter.

If you can rebuke the fear that is knocking at the door of your heart, and tell that low self-esteem it cannot come in, and rebuke all the spirits that are waiting to attack you and make you captive, you are Sarah's daughter.

If you can stand calm in the midst of the storm and say, "I know God will deliver me," you are Sarah's daughter. If you can walk with God in the midst of the storm and trust Him to bring you through dry places, you are Sarah's daughter.

If you can judge God faithful, and know that God cannot lie, understanding that satan is the father of lies, you are Sarah's daughter.

If you can stand there when fear is trying to get you to overreact and fall apart, you are Sarah's daughter. If you can stand there and push a tear from off the side of your face and smile in the middle of the rain, you are Sarah's daughter.

God is adorning you with glory, power, and majesty. He will send people into your life to appreciate your real beauty, your real essence. It is the kind of beauty that lasts despite a face full of wrinkles, gray hair, falling arches, crow's feet, and all the pitfalls that may come your way. There's a beauty that you can see in a 90-year-old woman's face that causes an old man to smile. God is decorating you on the inside. He is putting a glory in you that will shine through your eyes. A man will come along and look in your eyes. He will not talk about whether they were blue or whether your eye shadow was right or not. He will look in your eyes and see trust, peace, love, and life.

YOUR HEALING JOURNEY

You are not designed to react to circumstances; God wants to raise you up to become someone circumstances react to. This is why you need to guard your interior life. More than who you are, it's how you respond. How you react. These expressions need to reflect your inner beauty as well. In fact, the interior life is most authentically revealed under pressure. We see this time after time in examples in Scripture. Faith or fear comes to the surface when a man, woman, or people group is faced with challenging odds.

So how do you react? Do you behave as a daughter of Sarah—because this is who you are! Just as we have "Father Abraham," we could say that we have "Mother Sarah." She played a significant role in the unfolding of God's plan for humanity, as it was her womb that Heaven supernaturally graced with fertility to conceive Isaac long after it was naturally possible for her to have children.

Was Sarah perfect? Of course not. None of the great heroes and heroines of the faith were perfect. Quite the opposite in many cases. God does not use you based on your perfection; He uses you based on your belief and willingness to obey. Sarah obeyed God by believing Him, regardless of what circumstances came against her. Did she have seasons where she struggled? Yes! She even tried to help God out by giving her own husband, Abraham, to her maidservant, in hopes that she could give him the child of promise.

In the end, Sarah believed God. Maybe you tried to do God's job for Him in the past, bringing His purposes to pass through your good intentions. Perhaps that got you into trouble. Doesn't matter. The past is over. God wants to birth His divine purposes through you. What's the qualification? Simply believe Him. Model Sarah and judge the Lord who promised to be faithful!

Day Seventy

YOUR SABBATH REST

*And he was teaching in one of the synagogues on the
sabbath. And, behold, there was a woman which
had a spirit of infirmity eighteen years, and was
bowed together, and could in no wise lift up herself.*
—LUKE 13:10-11

It is not a mere coincidence that this woman was healed
on the Sabbath day. The Bible goes to great pains to make
us aware that it was during the Sabbath that this woman
experienced her healing.

The Sabbath is a day of rest. It is a day of restoration.
Following creation, on the seventh day God rested (see Gen.
2:2-3). Rest is for the purpose of restoration. It is not just
because you're tired. It is during a time of rest that you
replenish or receive back those things that were expended or
put out. It is during the time of restoration that the enemy
wants to break off your fellowship with the Lord.

I don't want you to think of rest just in terms of sleep. Please
understand that rest and restoration are related concepts. The

enemy does not want you to have rest. You need calmness or Sabbath rest because it is through the resting of your spirit that the restoration of your life begins to occur.

The Sabbath was meant not only for God to rest, but also for God to enjoy His creation with man. The issues are rest and communion.

In the nation of Israel, God used the Sabbath day as a sign of the covenant. It proved that they were His people. They spent time in worship and fellowship with the Lord. That is the Sabbath. It is real communion between the heart of man and heart of God.

When Jesus began to minister in a restful situation, needs began to be manifested. The infirm woman's need was revealed in the midst of the Sabbath. You can never get your needs met by losing your head. When you calm down, God speaks.

When you start murmuring and complaining, the only thing God can focus on is your unbelief. When you start resting in Him, He can focus on your problems and on the areas of your life that need to be touched.

When you begin to enter into real worship with God, that's the best time to have Him minister to your needs. That's the time God does restoration in your life. Satan, therefore, wants to break up your Sabbath rest.

The infirm woman was not sitting around complaining. She was not murmuring. She was not hysterical. She had a problem, but she was calm. She was just sitting there listening to the words of the Master. She brought her problem with her, but her problem had not dominated her worship.

YOUR HEALING JOURNEY

Embrace rest and restoration! In order to receive healing, you need to slow down. Give yourself permission to enjoy a Sabbath rest. Is there a specific day that you want to offer up to the Lord as a designated day of rest? If life affords you the ability to do this, by all means—go ahead!

However, as we read deeper in the New Testament, we quickly discover that the Sabbath is not about a special day; it's about a whole new realm of living. Jesus made it possible for you to enter a lifelong Sabbath rest.

No, this doesn't mean you are excused from the everyday duties of life, but it does mean you can rest from your striving. You can rest from trying to earn God's love and God's favor. You can rest from trying to clean yourself up in order for God to work with you. You can rest from trying to fix, change, and adjust the people in your life. Recognize that you are incapable of doing any of these things with any measure of success. And that's okay! Lay these things before the Lord and simply behold Jesus, the personification of Sabbath Rest!

He knew that you could not fulfill the rules and regulations to become acceptable to God, so He did it for you. Rest in His completed work. Take a deep breath. The message of the Cross still resounds loud and clear today: "It is finished!"

Day Seventy-One

PRESS INTO THE REST FOUND IN JESUS

*Come unto me, all ye that labour and are heavy
laden, and I will give you rest. Take my yoke upon
you, and learn of me; for I am meek and lowly
in heart: and ye shall find rest unto your souls.
For my yoke is easy, and my burden is light.*
—MATTHEW 11:28-30

I want to zoom in on the Sabbath day because what the
Sabbath was physically, Christ is spiritually. Christ is our
Sabbath rest. He is the end of our labors. We are saved by
grace through faith and not by works, lest any man should
be able to boast (see Eph. 2:8-9).

The rest of the Lord is so complete that when Jesus was
dying on the Cross, He said, *"It is finished"* (John 19:30). It
was so powerful. For the first time in history, a high priest sat
down in the presence of God without having to run in and
out bringing blood to atone for the sins of man. When Christ

entered in once and for all, He offered up Himself for us that we might be delivered from sin.

If you really want to be healed, you've got to be in Him. If you really want to be set free and experience restoration, you've got to be in Him because your healing comes in the Sabbath rest. Your healing comes in Christ Jesus. As you rest in Him, every infirmity, every area bent out of place will be restored.

The devil knows this truth, so he does not want you to rest in the Lord. Satan wants you to be anxious. He wants you to be upset. He wants you to be hysterical. He wants you to be suicidal, doubtful, fearful, and neurotic.

> *There remaineth therefore a rest to the people of God. For he that is entered into his rest, he also hath ceased from his own works, as God did from his. Let us labour therefore to enter into that rest, lest any man fall after the same example of unbelief* (Hebrews 4:9-11).

Sometimes it takes work to find the place of rest and calm. Our hectic world does not lend itself to quiet and peace. It creates noise and uneasiness. Even though the infirm woman was bowed over and could not lift herself, she rested in the fact that she was in the presence of a mighty God. He is able to do exceedingly and abundantly above all that we may ask or think (see Eph. 3:20).

YOUR HEALING JOURNEY

Yes, you need to work for your Sabbath rest. It sounds counterintuitive, but consider some of the practical factors you are dealing with. The world is noisy. "Busy" is quickly becoming a standard greeting response these days. "How are you doing?" "Busy!"

It takes concentrated effort for you to find a place of rest and calm. The culture of our world is the exact opposite to this. So, what do you do?

Make a dedicated decision that you will not allow the noise outside to impact your inside. You have to exercise your will not to allow everything going on around you to affect what's going on in you. As you do this, you will watch an unusual ability develop. You will walk in the very solution that a situation needs. Crisis doesn't knock you off course; in fact, the atmosphere of peace and rest within you is the very thing that people in crisis need to stabilize. Rather than being changed by the atmosphere around you, you start to change the atmosphere because of the interior standards you hold.

You are willing to fight for the position of rest. It's non-negotiable! And when you live from this place, the world will take notice and long for the grace you walk in.

Day Seventy-Two

REST IN YOUR IDENTITY

Jesus answered and said unto her, Whosoever drinketh of this water shall thirst again: but whosoever drinketh of the water that I shall give him shall never thirst; but the water that I shall give him shall be in him a well of water springing up into everlasting life.
—JOHN 4:13-14

Jesus confronted the woman at the well with some exciting truths. He was sitting at the well waiting for someone to return. He was relaxed. He was calm and resting. He knew who He was. God doesn't get excited about circumstances.

Another time the disciples and Jesus were on a ship. A storm arose and appeared to be about to sink the ship. However, Jesus didn't become concerned about circumstances. In fact, He was sleeping, resting in the middle of a crisis. Everyone else was running all over the boat trying to figure out how they would get into life jackets and into the lifeboats. Was Jesus resting because He was lazy? No, He was resting because He knew He was greater than the storm. Jesus rose up and spoke to the winds and waves and said, *"Peace, be still"* (Mark 4:39).

When you know who you are, you don't have to struggle. You don't have to wake Him up.

YOUR HEALING JOURNEY

When you know that you are secure in Christ, you can rest—anytime, anywhere. Of course storms will arise that try to shake everything around you. Such comes with the territory of living in this world. Storms are common; what's uncommon is the woman who remains steadfast in the storm.

How is this possible? When you know who you are, you can rest unshaken by what's going on around you. After all, if God has made certain pronouncements and promises concerning you—which He has throughout the Scriptures—then nothing life throws your way can unsettle you. You may shake. You may cry. You may feel...and feel strongly. But one thing you will not be is thrown off course. You are a woman on a mission. You have been healed, loosed, and delivered. The Master called you, He cleaned you, and He commissioned you. Nothing can change those truths!

ENTER THE HEALING REST OF JESUS'S PRESENCE

*The woman saith unto him, Sir, give me
this water, that I thirst not, neither come
hither to draw. Jesus saith unto her, Go,
call thy husband, and come hither.*
—JOHN 4:15-16

When this woman came down with her waterpot on her shoulder, she was all upset and worried about the water she needed to draw. Jesus was sitting by the well. He began to demonstrate calmness. He told her, "If you drink of the water that you have, you will thirst again, but if you drink of the water that I have, you will never thirst." But then, Jesus shifted the focus of the conversation to the real need.

*The woman answered and said, I have no husband.
Jesus said unto her, Thou hast well said, I have no
husband: for thou hast had five husbands; and he*

whom thou now hast is not thy husband: in that saidst thou truly (John 4:17-18).

Like this woman, you can get yourself into situations that wound and upset your spirit. These kinds of wounds can't be healed through human effort. You must get in the presence of God and let Him fill those voids in your life. You will not settle it up by going from friend to friend. This woman had already tried that. She had already gone through five men. The answer is not getting another man. It's getting in touch with *the Man—Jesus.*

The woman at the well threw down her waterpot and ran to tell others about the Man she had met at the well. We too need to get rid of the old, carnal man. Some of those old attachments and old ways of living need to be replaced with the calmness of the Spirit.

This woman could never have rid herself of the old man until she met the new Man. When you meet the new, you get the power to say good-bye to the old. You will never be able to break the grip on your life that those old ways have until you know Jesus Christ is the real way. You will never get it straight without Jesus. You must come to Him just as you are. Knowing Him will give you the power to break away from the old self and the ties that bind.

YOUR HEALING JOURNEY

Expect to receive wholeness as you rest in the presence of Jesus. In fact, take this moment to grow quiet before the Lord.

Let His presence wash over you like a restoring healing balm.

Thank Him for being present.

Thank Him for promising never to leave you or forsake you.

Thank Him for providing rest for you through the Cross. You can pray,

Lord, I receive the healing rest of Jesus. Right now, I surrender. Holy Spirit, wash over me. Wash over my soul. Every area of my life that needs Your touch, I invite You in. I give You control.

Ask the Lord to show you any areas that you might be holding on to—specifically, matters of control. He wants to help you break this, as the drive for control is one of the greatest hindrances to experiencing His peace and rest.

ONE ENCOUNTER THAT CHANGES YOUR DIRECTION IN LIFE

*The woman then left her waterpot, and went
her way into the city, and saith to the men,
Come, see a man, which told me all things
that ever I did: is not this the Christ?*
—JOHN 4:28-29

If you have something that has attached itself to you that is not of God, you won't be able to break it through your own strength. Submit yourself unto God, resist the enemy, and he will flee from you (see James 4:7). As you submit to God, you receive the power to resist the enemy.

The woman at the well didn't even go back home. She ran into the city telling everyone to come and see the Man who had told her about her life. You do yourself a disservice until you really come to know Jesus. He satisfies. Everyone else, well, they pacify, but Jesus satisfies. He can satisfy every need and every yearning. He heals every pain and every affliction. Then He lifts every burden and every trouble in your life.

You have had enough tragedy. You have been bent over long enough. God will do something good in you. God kept you living through all those years of infirmity because He had something greater for you than what you've experienced earlier. God kept you because He has something better for you.

You may have been abused and misused. Perhaps all those you trusted in turned on you and broke your heart. Still God has sustained you. You didn't make it because you were strong. You didn't make it because you were smart. You didn't make it because you were wise. You made it because God's amazing grace kept you and sustained you. God has more for you today than what you went through yesterday. Don't give up. Don't give in. Hold on. The blessing is on the way.

YOUR HEALING JOURNEY

I dare you to realize that you can do all things through Christ who strengthens you (see Phil. 4:13). Once the infirm woman knew that she didn't have to be bent over, she stood straight up. Jesus told the woman at the well to get rid of the old. He wanted her to step away from that old pattern of selfishness. Suddenly, she recognized that she didn't have what she thought she had. The sinful things that you have fought to maintain are not worth what you thought they were.

Day Seventy-Five

IT'S NOT TOO LATE!

*And Ruth said, Intreat me not to leave thee, or to
return from following after thee: for whither thou
goest, I will go; and where thou lodgest, I will lodge:
thy people shall be my people, and thy God my God.*
—RUTH 1:16

Ruth was Naomi's daughter-in-law. Naomi thought their
only connection was her now-dead son. Many times we, who
have been very family oriented, do not understand friendships.
When family circumstances change, we lapse into isolation
because we know nothing of other relationships. There are
bonds that are stronger than blood (see Prov. 18:24). They are
God-bonds! When God brings someone into our life, He is
the bonding agent.

Ruth said, "Your God shall be my God." God wanted
Naomi to see the splendor of winter relationships, the joy of
passing the baton of her wisdom and strength to someone
worthy of her attention. We need to let God choose such a
person for us because too often we choose on the basis of
fleshly ties and not godly ties. I have noticed in the Scriptures

that the strongest female relationships tend to be exemplified between older and younger women. I am certainly not suggesting that such will always be the case. However, let me submit a few cases for your own edification.

- Ruth would have died in Moab, probably marrying some heathen idolater if it were not for the wisdom of Naomi, an older, more seasoned woman. Naomi knew how to provide guidance without manipulation—a strength many women at Ruth's stage of life do not have. Ruth was, of course, one of the great-grandparents in the lineage of Jesus Christ. She had greatness in her that God used Naomi to cultivate. Perhaps Naomi would have been called Mara and perhaps she would have ended up dying in bitterness instead of touching lives if it had not been for Ruth.

- Elisabeth, the wife of the priest Zacharias, is the biblical synonym for the modern pastor's wife. She was a winter woman with a summer experience. She was pregnant with a promise. In spite of her declining years, she was fulfilling more destiny then than she had in her youth. She is biblical proof that God blesses us in His own time and on His own terms. She was also in seclusion. Perhaps it was the attitude of the community. Many times when an older woman is still vibrant and productive it can cause jealousy and intimidation. Perhaps it was the silent stillness in her womb which some believe she experienced. Whatever the reason, she was a recluse for six months until she heard a knock at the door. If you have isolated yourself from others, regardless of the reason, I pray you will hear the knocking of the Lord. He will give you the garment of praise to clothe the spirit of heaviness (see Isa. 61:3).

When Elisabeth lifted her still-creaking body, which seemed almost anchored down to the chair, and drug her enlarged torso to the door, she saw a young girl, a picture of herself in days gone by, standing there. Opening that door changed her life forever.

YOUR HEALING JOURNEY

As you open the door to new relationships and remove the chain from your own fears, God will overwhelm you with new splendor. Mary, the future mother of our Savior and Lord, Elisabeth's young cousin, was at the door. The salutation of this young woman, the exposure to her experience, made the baby in Elisabeth's womb leap and Elisabeth was filled with the Holy Ghost. God will jump-start your heart! He doesn't mean for you to go sit in a chair and die! In Jesus's name, get up and answer the door! People probably wondered why these women were so close who were so different, but it was a God-bond!

GOD PROMISED TO RESTORE YOU...AND HE WILL!

He restoreth my soul.
—PSALM 23:3

While I was in school, I worked at a local paint store. I had to acquaint myself with the products and procedures. I was intrigued by a refinishing product that restored old furniture to its former luster. I purchased the product to see if it was as effective as I had been told. I learned right away that the most difficult part of restoring furniture was stripping off the old wax.

It takes patience to overcome the effects of years of use and abuse. If you are not committed to getting back what you once had, you could easily decide that the process is impossible. Nevertheless, I assure you it is not impossible. David, the psalmist, declares, *"He restoreth my soul"* (Ps. 23:3). The term *restoreth* is a process. Only God knows what it takes to remove the build-up that may be existing in your life. But He specializes in restoring and renewing the human heart.

And the women said unto Naomi, Blessed be the Lord, which hath not left thee this day without a kinsman, that his name may be famous in Israel. And he shall be unto thee a restorer of thy life, and a nourisher of thine old age: for thy daughter in law, which loveth thee, which is better to thee than seven sons, hath born him (Ruth 4:14-15).

Naomi almost changed her name to Mara. She felt that God had dealt very bitterly with her. It is dangerous to be prejudiced against God. Prejudice is to pre-judge. People, even believers, have often prejudged God. However, He isn't finished yet. Before it was over, everyone agreed that the hand of the Lord was upon Naomi. Therefore, you are not off course.

YOUR HEALING JOURNEY

Trust God to see you through days that may be different from the ones you encountered earlier. You are being challenged with the silent struggles of winter. I believe the most painful experience is to look backward and have to stare into the cold face of regret.

Most people have thought, "I wonder how things would have been had I not made this decision or that one." To realize that you have been the victim and the assailant in your own life may be difficult to accept—especially because most of those dilemmas are birthed through the womb of your own decisions. Admittedly, there are those who inadvertently crashed into circumstances that stripped them, wounded them, and left them feeling like the victim on the Jericho road! (See Luke 10:30.)

No matter which case best describes your current situation, first pause and thank God that, like Naomi, in spite of the tragedies of youth it is a miracle that you survived the solemn chill of former days. Your presence should be a praise. Look over your shoulder and see what could have been. Has God dealt with you bitterly? I think not.

THE LORD, YOUR RESTORER

*And I will restore to you the years that the locust
hath eaten, the cankerworm, and the caterpillar,
and the palmerworm, my great army which I
sent among you. And ye shall eat in plenty, and
be satisfied, and praise the name of the Lord
your God, that hath dealt wondrously with
you: and my people shall never be ashamed.*
—JOEL 2:25-26

Anyone can recognize Him in the sunshine, but in the storm
His disciples thought He was a ghost (see Matt. 14:26).

There are two things every Naomi can rely upon as she
gathers wood for winter days and wraps quilts around weak,
willowy legs: *God is a restorer.* That is to say, as you sit by
the fire sipping coffee, rehearsing your own thoughts, playing
old reruns from the scenes in your life—some things He will
explain and others He will heal. Restoration doesn't mean
all the lost people who left you will return. Neither Naomi's

husband nor her sons were resurrected. It is just that God gives purpose back to the years that had question marks.

How many times have you been able to look back and say, "If I hadn't gone through that, I wouldn't have known or received this"? Simply said, "He'll make it up to you." He restores the effects of the years of turmoil.

People who heard Naomi running through the house with rollers in her hair complaining that God had dealt bitterly should have waited with their noses pressed against the windowpane as God masterfully brought peace into her arms.

If you wait by the window, you will hear the soft hum of an old woman nodding with her grandchild clutched in her arms. Perhaps she is too proud to tell you that she charged God foolishly, but the smile on her leathery face and the calmness of her rest says, *"He hath done all things well"* (Mark 7:37).

YOUR HEALING JOURNEY

God is a Restorer. You might be familiar with this concept. But really reflect on it for a moment. When God restores, He makes something better than it was to begin with. When He restored mankind, His restoration process made something possible that was not even available in Eden.

In the Garden of Eden, God walked with man. Now, because of Jesus's blood and the indwelling Holy Spirit, God walks **in** man. When you walk, God walks. Where you walk, God walks. God lives inside of you. This is the greatest demonstration of His identity as the Restoring God.

Take this opportunity to ask the Lord to point out areas in your past that need His restoring touch. Whether it was the result of your own poor choice or the offense of someone else toward you, God's desire is to restore the effects of past trauma.

THE LORD, YOUR NOURISHER

I will refresh the weary and satisfy the faint.
—JEREMIAH 31:25, NIV

The Lord will also be known as *the nourisher*. This may be a difficult role for you who have clutched babies and men alike to the warm breast of your sensitivity. You, who have been the source for others to be strengthened, may find it difficult to know what to do with this role reversal. The nourisher must learn to be nourished.

Many women pray more earnestly as intercessors for others than for themselves. That is wonderful, but there ought to be a time when you desire certain things for yourself. Our God is El Shaddai, "the breasted one" (from Gen. 17:1). He gives strength to the feeble and warmth to the cold. There is great comfort in His arms. Like children, even adults can snuggle into His everlasting arms and hear the heartbeat of a loving God who says, "*And ye shall eat in plenty, and be satisfied, and praise the name of the Lord your God*" (Joel 2:26).

YOUR HEALING JOURNEY

God wants to nourish you. He wants to satisfy you. Yes, you!

Even though people are often quick to emphasize the "work of ministry" where Christians are encouraged to demonstrate the kindness of Jesus to others, the truth is the "givers" also need to receive nourishment.

You need to receive in order to give. If you find the process imbalanced in your life, where you are giving, giving, giving all the time, you will be well on your way to burnout. Don't let it get to that point! Give to others freely, but also be intentional and give to yourself. Love yourself. Nourish yourself.

The Lord wants to refresh you so you can effectively bring His refreshing to others!

EXPECT HEAVEN'S ANGELS

Do not forget to show hospitality to strangers,
for by so doing some people have shown
hospitality to angels without knowing it.
—HEBREWS 13:2, NIV

Expect God in all His varied forms. He is a master of disguise, a guiding star in the night, a lily left growing in the valley, or an answered prayer sent on the breath of an angel. Angels are the butlers of Heaven; they open doors. He sends angels to minister to His own. Have you ever seen an angel? They aren't always dressed in white with dramatically arched wings. Sometimes they are so ordinary that they can be overlooked. Ruth was an angel Naomi almost sent away. God can use anyone as a channel of nourishment. Regardless of the channel, He is still the source.

When Hagar was lost in the wilderness of depression and wrestling exasperation, God sent an angel. When the labor-ridden mother of Samson was mundane and barren, God sent an angel. When young Mary was wandering listlessly through life, God sent an angel. When the grief-stricken Mary Magdalene came stumbling down to the tomb, God sent an angel. For every woman in crisis, there is an angel! For every lonely night and forgotten mother, there is an angel. For every lost young girl wandering the concrete jungle of an inner city, there is an angel. My sister, set your coffee down, take the blanket off your legs, and stand up on your feet! Hast thou not known, hast thou not heard?

For every woman facing winter, *there is an angel!*

YOUR HEALING JOURNEY

Are not all angels ministering spirits sent to serve those who will inherit salvation? (Hebrews 1:14 NIV)

Through faith also Sara herself received strength to conceive seed, and was delivered of a child when she was past age, because she judged him faithful who had promised (Hebrews 11:11).

Angels are all around us! There is constant activity taking place in the spirit realm even as you read these words. Sometimes, the veil is peeled back ever so slightly so that those on earth are able to catch glimpses of those moving about in the heavenly places.

Trust that God dispatches His angels to you at the right time, in the right season. And be sure to consider those moments that one might label a coincidence. A chance meeting? A divine appointment? In God's economy, there are no coincidences. You serve a God of purpose.

Heaven's agenda is unfolding day after day. Be confident knowing that God's will for your life is being executed by angelic messengers!

GET READY TO LAUGH
WITH GOD

*Sarah became pregnant and bore a son to Abraham
in his old age, at the very time God had promised
him. Abraham gave the name Isaac to the son Sarah
bore him. When his son Isaac was eight days old,
Abraham circumcised him, as God commanded
him. Abraham was a hundred years old when his
son Isaac was born to him. Sarah said, "God has
brought me laughter, and everyone who hears about
this will laugh with me." And she added, "Who
would have said to Abraham that Sarah would nurse
children? Yet I have borne him a son in his old age."*
—GENESIS 21:2-7, NIV

I think it would be remiss of me not to share, before
moving on, the miracles of winter. In the summer, all was
well with Sarah. At that time she knew little about Jehovah,
her husband's God. She basically knew she was in love with
a wonderful man. She was the luckiest woman in Ur. An

incredibly beautiful woman already, she wore her love like a striking woman wears a flattering dress. The air smelled like honeysuckle and the wind called her name. Then her husband spoke to her about moving. Where, she didn't know, and crazy as it may sound to those who have forgotten the excitement of summer, she really didn't care. She ran into the tent and began to pack. Sometimes it's good to get away from relatives and friends. Starting over would be fun!

Soon the giddy exuberance of summer started to ebb as she began wrestling with the harsh realities of following a dreamer. Abraham had not done what he said; he carried a few of their relatives with them. "I am sure he had a good reason," she thought. What was really troubling her wasn't the strife between the relatives or the fighting herdsmen, it was the absence of a child. By now she was sure she was barren. She felt like she had cheated Abraham out of an important part of life. Someone had said she would have a baby. Sarah laughed, "If I am going to get a miracle, God had better hurry."

I want to warn you against setting your own watch. God's time is not your time. He may not come when you want Him to, but He is right on time. Twice it is mentioned that Sarah laughed. The first time she laughed at God.

> *Abraham and Sarah were already very old, and Sarah was past the age of childbearing. So Sarah laughed to herself as she thought, "After I am worn*

out and my lord is old, will I now have this plea-
sure?" Then the Lord said to Abraham, "Why did
Sarah laugh and say, 'Will I really have a child,
now that I am old?' Is anything too hard for the
Lord? I will return to you at the appointed time
next year and Sarah will have a son" (Genesis
18:11-14 NIV).

However, in the winter time she laughed *with* God. The
first time she laughed at the impossibility of God's promise.
After she had gone through life's experiences, she learned that
God is faithful to perform His word.

YOUR HEALING JOURNEY

Get ready to laugh with God!

Why are you going to laugh with Him? Because where
you're going far exceeds where you've been.

Take a moment to reflect on your journey so far. It's important to remind yourself of the great works the Lord has
performed in your life. Once you start, it's difficult to stop.

Consider what He brought you out of and what He
brought you through.

Bring to your remembrance every answered prayer and
midnight hour miracle.

As you remember what He did, you are setting your level
of expectation. The God who moved in your life will surely
move again. And as He moves, you will laugh with Him.

You will rejoice, looking at where you are and measuring it beside where you came from.

Surely, all you will be able to say is, "Look what the Lord has done!"

Day Eighty-One

PERSEVERING THROUGH THE PROCESS

*And by faith even Sarah, who was past childbearing
age, was enabled to bear children because she
considered him faithful who had made the promise.*
—HEBREWS 11:11, NIV

Often we share our personal testimony. We tell where
we started and even where we ultimately arrived without
sharing the process or the sequence of events that led to our
deliverance. Then our listeners feel defeated because they
named it and claimed it and still didn't attain it! We didn't
tell them about the awful trying of our faith that preceded
our coming forth as pure gold. Today, however, we will share
the whole truth and nothing but the truth! Amen.

In between these powerful moments in the life of one of
God's finest examples of wives (Sarah), everything in her was
tested. I believe that her love for Abraham gave her the courage to leave home, but her love for God brought forth the
promised seed.

YOUR HEALING JOURNEY

Consider your Lord faithful. The steadfast truth of His faithfulness will enable you to persevere through any process, any storm, and any season.

The secret to Sarah's miracle was how she considered the Lord. So let me ask you this question: How do you consider the Lord?

Is He faithful? Or are you concerned that He's going to bail out on you?

Is He trustworthy? Or do you see God like you saw a man or a friend who proved to be less than reliable?

YOUR GOD WILL NOT FORSAKE YOU!

*Though my father and mother forsake
me, the Lord will receive me.*
—PSALM 27:10, NIV

In summer, Sarah followed Abraham out of their country and away from their kindred. As the seasons of life change, she takes another pilgrimage into what could have been a great tragedy. Abraham, her beloved husband, leads his wife into Gerar. As I am a man and a leader myself, I dare not be too hard on him. Anyone can make a poor decision. The decision to go to Gerar I could defend, even though Gerar means "halting place."

I have made decisions that brought me to a halting place in my life. What's reprehensible is that Abraham, Sarah's protector and covering, when afraid for his own safety lied about her identity (see Gen. 20). You never know who people are until you witness them under pressure. Now, I am not being sanctimonious about Abraham's flagrant disregard for truth. But it was a life-threatening lie.

Have you ever known someone upon whom you had cast the weight of your confidence, only to have your trust defrauded in a moment when that person acted in self-gratification and indulgence? Someone who has a selfish need can jeopardize all that you have. Abraham's infamous lie jeopardized the safety of his wife. King Abimelech was a heathen king. He was used to getting whatever he wanted. His reputation for debauchery preceded him to the degree that Abraham, the father of faith, feared for his life. Rather than risk himself, he told the king that his lovely wife was really his sister. Abraham knew that such a statement would cause Sarah to have to fulfill the torrid desires of a heathen. Sarah now finds herself being bathed and perfumed to be offered up as an offering of lust for the passions of the king. Imagine the icy grip of fear clutching the first lady of faith. Imagine her shock to realize that under real stress, a person can never be sure what another individual will do to secure his own well-being.

YOUR HEALING JOURNEY

Sarah's Abraham failed her. But God did not!

Maybe there is someone in your life who selfishly threw you into a tempestuous situation. Take courage! Just because satan has set a snare doesn't mean you can't escape. The God we serve is able. His word to you is, "Woman, thou art loosed."

Day Eighty-Three

GREAT IS THY FAITHFULNESS

*Great is his faithfulness; his mercies
begin afresh each morning.*
—LAMENTATIONS 3:23, NLT

When Sarah came out of Gerar, she knew something about life, about people, and most of all about God. She didn't lose her relationship with Abraham, as we will soon see. But she did learn something that all of us must learn too. She learned the faithfulness of God.

I am convinced that the things that worry us would not if we knew the faithfulness of God. Have you ever spent the night in a Gerar situation? If you have, you know the Lord in a way you could never know Him otherwise. He cares for you! Look over your past and remember His faithfulness. Look at your future and trust Him now!

YOUR HEALING JOURNEY

Take a moment to reflect on what God has delivered you out of. It's easy to get so preoccupied with our present struggles that we fail to offer up thanks for how far we've come in our journey so far.

It might be inches; it may be miles. Progress is progress, and God wants to lead His people into a triumphal procession. Onward and forward! Glory to glory. Strength to strength.

The goal is to be able to look back on the past and instead of pain see purpose. Did God orchestrate the horrible thing that happened to you? Certainly not. Did God cause you to make the poor decision that changed your life dramatically…and for the worse? No. God is not the author of evil; however, He works in the midst of it. Evil does not come from God, but evil does not restrain the movement of God either. His light can break forth even in the darkest night.

As you finish your journey, take some time to reflect on how you saw God working, even in the midst of the dark times of your past. Chances are, after prayerfully considering it, you will begin to see evidence of divine movement in your life all along the journey. Even when you were in the deepest pit, surely you will note the familiar trace of His presence. In some way, shape, or form, God was right there with you.

Be encouraged knowing that your God is faithful through and through!

YOUR LIFE SOURCE

*And the Lord visited Sarah as he had said, and the
Lord did unto Sarah as he had spoken. For Sarah
conceived, and bare Abraham a son in his old age,
at the set time of which God had spoken to him.*
—GENESIS 21:1-2

It wasn't Abraham's visit to the tent that left that woman
filled with the promise of God. Without God he could do
nothing. Always remember that man may be the instrument,
but God is the life source. It was God who visited Sarah.
Now Sarah knew God like she had never known Him. Some
things you can learn about God only in the winter. Sarah
won a spot in the hallmark of faith.

When Hebrews chapter 11 lists the patriarchs and their
awesome faith, this winter woman's name is included. Abraham is mentioned for the kind of faith that would leave home
and look for a city whose builder and maker is God (see Heb.
11:10).

But when it comes to discussing the kind of faith that caused an old woman's barren womb to conceive, it was Sarah's faith that did it (see Heb. 11:11).

YOUR HEALING JOURNEY

Sarah didn't take faith classes. She just went through her winter clutching the warm hand of a loving God who would not fail. So when you hear Sarah laughing the last time, she is laughing with God. She is holding her baby to her now wrinkled breast. She understands the miracles that come only to winter women.

Day Eighty-Five

GOD DESIRES YOU

Don't be afraid, I've redeemed you. I've called your name. You're mine. When you're in over your head, I'll be there with you. When you're in rough waters, you will not go down. When you're between a rock and a hard place, it won't be a dead end—because I am God, your personal God, the Holy of Israel, your Savior.
—ISAIAH 43:1-3, MSG

There is awesome power in women. God has chosen that women serve as the vehicles through which entry is made into this world. He has shared His creativity with women. Women are strong and willing to nurture others.

In spite of this, millions of women continually suffer emotional, physical, and spiritual strain. The enemy has attempted to destroy God's vehicle of creativity.

You may be one of those who suffer. Perhaps you sit and wonder whether life will ever be normal for you. Maybe you feel like your circumstance has made you different from other women. You feel like you are alone, with no one to help you find healing.

It could be that your emotional strain comes from having been abused. Others have taken advantage of you and used you in the most horrible and depraved ways. You are left feeling used and dirty. How could anyone want someone who has been abused? Nevertheless, you are wanted. God wants you, and God's people want you.

YOUR HEALING JOURNEY

God does not simply tolerate you; He passionately desires you. He takes great delight in you! You were not His second choice; you are His prized possession. Know this.

As a woman who is set on course to walk in the wholeness and healing of Heaven, perhaps there is no greater truth to live mindful of then this—the Holy God loves you with an everlasting love.

Perhaps we have reduced the magnitude of God's love by talking about it without awe and wonder. But it should never cease to take our breath away.

God chose you. He handpicked you. He wanted you. He set His eye on you! And remember, God sees outside of time, so He choose you in spite of everything you did and everything you didn't do. He chose you regardless of your successes or failures. He came running toward you, even when you were running away from Him.

The Lord found it fit to redeem you and make you His own. You are a treasure to Him. Start seeing yourself this way. Start believing it's true. Some worry about inflated ego or imbalanced self-confidence. Trust me, you quit worrying about such things when you measure God's unconditional love toward you next to what you deserve. After all, you know yourself better than anyone else on earth. You know all of your deepest, darkest secrets. You know everything about yourself that you would never want anyone else knowing for fear that you would be humiliated, shamed, exposed.

Think of everything you know about yourself. Now, consider the fact that God knows all of this too. In fact, He knows you on an infinitely deeper level than you know yourself. And He loves you! He accepts you. He cherishes you. He rejoices over you!

Day Eighty-Six

BEHOLD YOUR REDEEMER

"Come now, let us settle the matter," says the
Lord. "Though your sins are like scarlet, they
shall be as white as snow; though they are
red as crimson, they shall be like wool."
—ISAIAH 1:18, NIV

Mistakes made early in life impact the rest of our lives.
Some become involved sexually without the commitment of
marriage. Maybe you believed him when he told you that he
loved you. Perhaps you really did think that yielding would
show your true love. Or maybe, you simply wanted to have a
good time without thinking about the consequences. You too
feel less than normal.

God has determined your need. He looked down from
Heaven and saw your pain and guilt. He evaluated the situation and decided that you needed a Redeemer. You need
Someone to reach down and lift you. He saw that you needed
to recognize how important you are. It is impossible to know
all that was in the mind of God when He looked down on

broken humanity, but we know He looked past our broken hearts, wounded histories, and our tendency to sin and saw our need.

He met that need through Jesus Christ. Jesus took your abuse on Himself on the Cross of Calvary. He paid for your shame. He made a way for you to be clean again. He took your indiscretions and sins upon Himself and died in your place. He saw your desire to please others and feel good. Thus, He took all your sinful desires and crucified them on the Cross.

YOUR HEALING JOURNEY

In spite of your mistakes, sins, failures, and past, God still looked down from Heaven with burning eyes of love and considered you worthy of redemption. Behold Him anew today.

We frequently use the term "Redeemer" when it comes to the identity of Jesus, but it's one thing to identify Him with a title; it's another dimension to encounter Him in this identity. Today, draw near to the Redeemer. Remember, He loves you. As John 3:16 reminds, God so loved you that He sent His only Son, Jesus, to bridge the gulf between you and Him. Your sins separated you from His perfection and His holiness. Yet He made a way to reach out to you. To reconnect with you. He redeemed you to Himself. He paid the highest price in eternity to purchase your salvation and make you His daughter forever.

When you behold your Redeemer, you recognize that the stain of your sin has been washed as white as snow. What a reason to give Him praise!

PAID IN FULL AT CALVARY

Yet now he has reconciled you to himself
through the death of Christ in his physical body.
As a result, he has brought you into his own
presence, and you are holy and blameless as
you stand before him without a single fault.
—COLOSSIANS 1:22, NLT

When you accept Jesus, you become clean and holy. You are made pure. Don't think you were alone, though; everyone struggles with the same kinds of sins as you, whether they show it on the outside or not.

The abused little girl with all her wounds was healed by the stripes of Jesus (see Isa. 53:5). The sins of the woman who wanted to fulfill her lusts were crucified on the Cross with Him (see Gal. 2:20). The past is paid for. The wounds may leave scars, but the scars are only there to remind us that we are human. Everyone has scars.

God recognizes the possibility of what you can become. He has a plan. He sees your potential. He also knows that your potential has been bound by your history. Your suffering made you into a different woman from the one He originally intended you to be. The circumstances of life shaped your way of thinking. The responses you made to those circumstances often kept you from living up to your potential.

YOUR HEALING JOURNEY

The transaction at the Cross was definitive. Final. "It is finished." Your sins, your past, your guilt, and your shame were paid in full at Calvary. Now what? Where do you go from there?

Linger a bit longer. Too many believers are quick to move past the Cross to get to the "next great teaching." Yet there is no revelation greater than or superior to the Cross. Why? You are a spiritual invalid apart from the saving work of Christ. Without His shed blood and the forgiveness of your sins, you cannot hear God's voice. You would not be able to understand the Bible, let alone any kind of preaching or teaching. You would have no relationship with God whatsoever. You would be blind and dead apart from the Cross, still imprisoned in your sins.

The problem is that due to our unwillingness to linger at the Cross, we move past its glory a little too quickly. We move past the finality of what Jesus accomplished on that wooden tree. Perhaps the devil would not be so successful at condemning Christ-followers if they had a greater vision of how deep the work of the Cross went in their lives. In their spirits. In their souls.

Through and through, the atoning work of Jesus delivered you from every sin, gave you power over every bondage, and brought you into right standing with the Holy God. You can face the past with confidence because all of it is under the blood of Jesus. No matter how great the sin or how deep the pain, Jesus's blood reaches to the highest heights and deepest depths. Simply receive it. Claim it. Praise Him for it.

It's a new day for you!

Day Eighty-Eight

LOOSED TO UNLOCK YOUR POTENTIAL!

You can show others the goodness of God, for he called you out of the darkness into his wonderful light.
—1 PETER 2:9, NLT

God knows that there is a Sarah, a Rahab, a woman at the well, a Ruth, or even a Mary in you. Hidden inside of you is a great woman who can do great exploits in His name. He wants that woman to be set free. He wants the potential within you to be unleashed so you can become the person you were created to be.

There is only one way to reach that potential. He is calling you. He will spiritually stir your heart and let you know that He is moving in your life, if you will only respond to His call.

The power to unleash you is in your faith. Dare to believe that He will do what He said He would do. Shift your confidence from your own weaknesses to His power. Trust in Him rather than in yourself. Anyone who comes to Christ will find deliverance and healing. He will soothe your wounds. He will comfort you in your desperate moments. He will raise you up.

YOUR HEALING JOURNEY

Believe that Jesus paid the price for your sin and guilt. Believe that He has washed you and made you clean. Believe that He will satisfy every need created by your history. Have faith that He will reward you when you call on Him, and it shall be done.

You have nothing to lose and everything to gain. Jesus will straighten the crooked places in your heart and make you completely whole. When you allow Him access to every area of your life, you will never be the same broken person again.

Day Eighty-Nine

Day Eighty-Nine

HIDDEN IN CHRIST

And, behold, there was a woman which had a spirit
of infirmity eighteen years, and was bowed together,
and could in no wise lift up herself. And when
Jesus saw her, he called her to him, and said unto
her, Woman, thou art loosed from thine infirmity.
And he laid his hands on her: and immediately
she was made straight, and glorified God.
—LUKE 13:11-13

We finish where we began—with the woman with a spirit of infirmity in Luke 13. For 18 years, she was defined by her condition. She was the *woman which had a spirit of infirmity.* Then, she met Jesus. One encounter with Him has the ability to dramatically shift identity.

To embrace the future, we must be willing to completely let go of the past. This means breaking agreement with our former identity. Some people are not willing to do this. They have become so familiar with that identity that they find it difficult to leave behind, even though it is destructive. The only reason

you hold on to a destructive identity is because you believe a lie. You are no longer one who makes agreements with the lies of the enemy. His tactics might have worked in the past, but they are going to prove absolutely futile in the days, weeks, months, and years ahead. Your identity is not in your condition. Your identity is not in your past. Your identity is not even in your husband, boyfriend, or significant other. Your identity is found in Christ. Paul the Apostle wrote that *"you have died, and your life is hidden with Christ in God"* (Col. 3:3, ESV).

Hide secure in your new identity. It's protection from the pain of the past.

In view of your journey up to this point, you should recognize the life-giving benefits of abandoning your previous, condition-assigned identity and embracing the healing words that proceed from the Savior's mouth. Let His words define you just as they defined the infirm woman in Luke 13.

YOUR HEALING JOURNEY

Don't be imprisoned by your past anymore. Start making these declarations of faith today and agree with your identity in Christ!

I am not defined by my sin; I am defined by the righteousness of God, which is in Christ Jesus. (see Rom. 3:22; 2 Cor. 5:21)

I am hidden in Christ! (see Col. 3:3)

It's no longer I who lives, but Christ who lives in me! (see Gal. 2:20)

I am dead to sin and alive to God in Christ Jesus! (see Rom. 6:11)

STEP INTO YOUR FUTURE!

*Therefore, if anyone is in Christ, he
is a new creation. The old has passed
away; behold, the new has come.*
—2 CORINTHIANS 5:17, ESV

Even though you have finished the 90-day journey, I recommend that you review back through this devotional on a regular basis. Freedom is not a quick fix. There are no shortcuts to walking in the liberty that Jesus provided. It's a daily journey.

Jesus wants you healed and whole in every area of your life. He came to set the captives free and loose those who were bound. For the woman free in Christ, there is no place for bondage. Your hands were not meant to be tied to the past; they were loosed to be extended in the air, responding in worship to the One who redeemed you and called you by name.

When the enemy of your soul tires to remind you of your past, agree with him. Yes, agree with him. Yes, you sinned.

Yes, you missed it. Yes, you made poor decisions that led to bondage. Yes, you entered destructive relationships. Yes, you were rejected. Yes, you were abandoned. Remember, the devil wants you to identify yourself based on his lies. Refuse to do it anymore!

Because of your boldness in Christ, you can agree 100 percent with the facts that the enemy presents before you. However, you proceed to remind him of the *higher truth.* Your past is completely covered by the precious blood of Jesus. Even your struggles and trials will be redeemed so that as you share out of your pain, you release healing to others. This completely reverses the enemy's strategy, backfiring on him.

As you move forward, I encourage you to remind yourself of your steadfast position in Christ. Nothing can shake you. Nothing can remove you from His firm, loving grasp. You are His. You are healed. You are whole.

Now, it's time to walk out your healing journey.

YOUR HEALING JOURNEY

Step confidently into your future and start making these declarations of faith today!

I am a new creation in Christ Jesus! The old is gone and the new is come! (see 2 Cor. 5:17; Rev. 21:5)

I am not imprisoned to my past anymore! (see Phil. 3:13-14)

The blood of Jesus has set me free from all sin, guilt, and shame! (see 1 John 1:7; Rev. 1:5)

I am healed and whole because of the work of the Cross! (see Isa. 53:5)

My identity is assigned by Christ—not the lies of the enemy or the expectations other people! (seePhil. 3:9)

Jesus set me free...and I am free indeed! (see John 8:36)

ABOUT T.D. JAKES

T.D. Jakes is a number-one *New York Times* best-selling author of more than 25 books. His ministry program, *The Potter's Touch*, is watched by 3.3 million viewers every week. He has produced Grammy Award-winning music and such films as *Heaven Is For Real, Sparkle*, and *Jumping the Broom*. A master communicator, he hosts Megafest, Woman Thou Art Loosed, and other conferences attended by tens of thousands.

Faithing It

THE FAITH FIGHT TO YOUR PURPOSE

Cora Jakes
COLEMAN

FREE E-BOOKS?
YES, PLEASE!

Get **FREE** and deeply-discounted **Christian books** for your **e-reader** delivered to your inbox **every week!**

IT'S SIMPLE!

VISIT lovetoreadclub.com

SUBSCRIBE by entering your email address

RECEIVE free and discounted e-book offers and inspiring articles delivered to your inbox every week!

Unsubscribe at any time.

SUBSCRIBE NOW!

LOVE TO READ CLUB

visit **LOVETOREADCLUB.COM** ▶